INVESTING
in a
WORLD
of
RISK

Duncan Stewart

The Author
Duncan Stewart has a background in compliance. He lives in Sydney, Australia.

First edition published by Heartflags Publishing, Sydney. Cover design by Heartflags Publishing.

National Library of Australia
Cataloguing-in-Publication entry

Author: Stewart, Duncan.

Title: Investing in a world of risk
                   / Duncan Stewart.

ISBN: 9780980552331 (pbk.)

Subjects: Investments.
                   Risk management.

Dewey Number: 332.6

Acknowledgements

I gratefully acknowledge the input of a number of people who reviewed parts of this book in its early stages:

Anita, Bronwyn, Cathy, Fadia and Spear.

Any mistakes that remain are, of course, entirely my own.

Disclaimer

Nothing in this book constitutes advice or is intended to be advice. No one should rely on this book to make investment decisions, whether they have purchased it or not. Readers should conduct their own research and form their own opinions before they make investment decisions. If readers have any doubts or questions, they should seek qualified and independent advice. The publisher and author expressly disclaim any liability, loss or risk that is incurred, directly or indirectly, as a result of the use and/or application of the contents of this book.

Contents

Introduction

I wrote *Investing in a World of Risk* against the background of a global financial crisis. That will be obvious to readers in 2010, but maybe not to those in future years. So I should say that the disaster featured easy credit, plus a boom in the housing and share markets. The boom built up over many years, but the collapse was sudden and severe. My thought was 'How can we stop it from happening again?' That is what this book is about, as well as regaining more of the confidence that underpins an economy.

A solution lies in the public outcry. It points to a whole group of people who were not to blame, but who could help to prevent another disaster. They have different talents that could be used. A challenge is to overcome any negative views that these people have about investing. Another challenge is that, whilst many already invest, they may have been taught strategies that do not suit them. It is possible that many investors have yet to reach their full potential.

This book sets out to make the most of the people and skills that we have in the community. To do so, we will look at investor behaviour and what makes up an individual's style. I use exaggerations about investors and their personalities to make this process easier. These descriptions are really just cartoons in the form of words. They are not based on real people. The idea is to look at some characteristics which you may recognise in others or even yourself. If you object, then what is the truth? Answer that and this book will still have succeeded at showing who we are.

The interesting thing about self-knowledge is the way in which risk is highlighted. Risk is what can go right or wrong in the future and surrounds every investor. How we respond to it is a function of our personality. Yet personalities differ, so there is not one strategy that is best. Instead, we each need to choose an investment strategy that suits our personality and approach to risk.

The effects of self-knowledge could be dramatic on a large scale. A wide range of risks may be matched more closely by the strategies of different investors. It could achieve the best balance between profit and loss, upside and downside risks. The result may be markets with fewer credit crunches or crashes, but law changes are necessary too.

In my opinion, laws should be used to encourage investors to apply their own investment style and strategy. This in turn should drive corporate behaviour. I will therefore make suggestions about how the law could be improved and encourage investors to get more involved. I have tried to simplify as much as I could, even if I go too far for some specialists.

A lot of ground is covered in this book and I want to make it as broadly applicable as possible. For this reason you may need to refer to more technical books in some areas. Or you may need to find out more about the laws and sharemarket rules in your country. An internet search could be a good starting point.

Last, I must point to a bias. I do not use market examples or quotes from famous successful investors. Many other books do that already. The problem is that readers may need to stop and check each example. Or they may trust some statistics or a quote taken out of context a little too much. I would prefer that you assess my ideas against what you know about yourself. In the end, my ambition is that you find your own path and follow it.

PART ONE
INVESTMENT STYLE

How To Use Part One

Investment style is the way in which you approach investment and your preferences. At the core of these preferences is simply your personality and risk tolerance. It affects how you respond to the risks of investment and which strategies will work best for you. Understanding yourself and so your investment style is the foundation of successful investing.

Use part one to understand:

- The four investment personalities:
    - Big Business
    - Intellectual
    - Small Business
    - Team Player

- What is risk? What is your liking for risk, or risk tolerance?

- Personality affects risk tolerance.

- Risk tolerance affects your investment decisions.

Be prepared to take a good look at yourself. Use your instincts to pick which of the investment personalities you most resemble. Does it *feel* right? Your answer will affect how you approach risk and investment.

Don't worry if your instincts seem to conflict with how you *think* you should be. Likewise, do not worry if your tolerance for risk seems to clash with your personality. This part is about finding out more about you. It is the start of improvement in how you invest.

Chapter One
Big Business

There are very few people who have a Big Business personality. Yet they seem to be held up as the ideal. Big Business people are often found as the leaders in companies and as entrepreneurs out on their own. They can be rich, so are an attractive subject to write about. But if they are still making their fortune then you might as well get out of their way because these people are in a hurry.

The Big Business personality is the master of the grand vision and how to realise it. These types are often company directors and chief executive officers, but also property developers, financiers and construction leaders. They will do what it takes and learn as much as they need to in order to succeed. As investors and leaders, Big Business types are energetic and decisive rather than clever. Their competitive side can also lead them to be intolerant of others with a different outlook on life. A Big Business personality who is making their way may therefore have little time for the less ambitious. Female Big Business types may view any reference to a 'glass ceiling' as a poor excuse for failure.[1] In fact, these people are so focused on their own goals that they may not accept those of others. If they bother to think about them at all.

Another side to their competitive nature is that some Big Business types may feel more like a winner if others lose. It may even create a need for never-ending challenges, whether in investment or other spheres. This contest and the organization that is required to win may suit the military mind, the politician or the bureaucrat who plays office politics without mercy.

---

1 "Glass ceiling" is used here to refer to invisible barriers to promotion, such as sexism.

Relationships

Big Business personalities are networkers with a purpose. They know their goals and size up opportunities to meet them through others. This can be as simple as inviting an expert out to lunch in order to learn something useful. Or they may seek out mentors who may also be able to guide them in future. The Big Business person is not shy if there is something useful to be learned or money to be made.

As a group, Big Business personalities will often flock together. They appreciate others with similar ideas and ambition. Plus Big Business people will be a good source of ideas, provided they have made their trades already. These contacts may be able to help each other one day, naturally.

I do not mean to suggest that Big Business people are venal, just that some may have more than one motive when they seek out others. Others might sniff at the superficial nature of these friendships, but Big Business types will accept them as part of the game that they play.

Whether the Big Business type wins or loses financially, it may be their old friends and family who suffer. Big Business types can jettison those who are no longer of any use. They are not heartless or lack a family orientation necessarily. It is just that they may have different goals and outgrow these relationships. A rising list of casualties will not stop the most ruthless who have limited remorse or guilt about their actions.

A kinder way of looking at the Big Business person is that they are not bound by the same rules as everyone else. How else would they have had the vision and courage to go against convention and build up capital before anyone else did? The Big Business personality can grab the moment and succeed before more worthy sorts have considered all the consequences. It may also mean that the Big Business people have a more simplified set of rules by which they act. It makes decisions that destroy relationships, like the dismissal of workers, so much easier.

Success

Big Business personalities may want symbols of success like a large salary, large team, a coveted corner office, a trophy spouse or an affair with the cute office junior that everyone knows about. Shopping can have a similar effect, but it is partly about the ability to spend, not what is bought. So the value of a symbol is for it advertises about the Big Business person and their achievements.

Someone I knew once made a mocking reference to the Big Business types and the size of their salaries. He thought he could do their job. If it is so easy, I said, then off you go. They can't all succeed just because of connections. There is nothing stopping you, except that the combination of personality and the skills needed are difficult to find.

In fact, the skill set needed to run a major corporation with many different businesses and markets is incredibly rare. You have to know enough about each of line of business to make good decisions and go out and represent your organisation to the community, shareholders, analysts and government. How many of these people do you know? Unless you have experience in a corporation it may be difficult to answer. But the rarer the person and the greater the demand for their skills, then the more they usually get paid in a free market, so these Big Business types gain wealth and all the symbols of success that they can stand.

In other cases, the Big Business type may meet their goals and it is still not enough. The lucky ones reach a cross-roads in their life and choose to go down another path. Their peers might dismiss them as having just a mid-life crisis, but the change can be more fundamental than that. A re-discovery of values can lead to a completely different set of goals. Some of the most financially successful may become philanthropists who use their skills to aid others. The same decisive energy that made them rich can be directed into charities with greater rewards that are not financial. Big Business types are therefore to be found in some unlikely and unexpected ventures helping the needy. Or they get involved in venture capital to bring new and useful technology to the world. Of course, some may short circuit this process and go straight to work on behalf of others in politics, regulators and charities. These Big Business types may have no time or interest in investment, or only to the extent that it funds their other plans.

Failure

If things go wrong and it is actually the Big Business personality who loses, then they may feel less hurt than many others in the same situation. Frustration, certainly, as they have less capital with which to invest. But the Big Business personality is not going to wallow in guilt and unhappiness for very long. Of all the people we will meet in this book, the Big Business personality is the most resilient. They are able to bounce back from adversity and try again. Failure for them is simply part of the game, of investing or doing business. If they are fortunate, the Big Business personality can identify what they did wrong and learn from it, even if it is only a quick private review.

Provided the mistakes did not involve criminality, a failed Big Business person can still be sought out by others. Usually like recognises like and people come together to work on common goals. The same notion appears to work for those high-flying company managers or politicians who seem to be picked from nowhere for promotion. Some people, without thinking too much about personality, assume there are favours or patronage involved. Perhaps there is, but please don't be too ready to assume it, particularly in the cut-throat world of business. Some who are already in leadership positions simply recognise the same personality and experience in others. The decision can be quick and as simple as a gut feeling.

A poor Big Business type in retirement is a sad sight. There is no fund to allow distressed entrepreneurs to start again. But these people may still have energy and decisiveness. Their frustration can make them prone to take risks in a rash attempt to catch up. Poverty may be the result, for it is a part of their rules that those who fail are allowed to do so.

Summary

It may seem that I have been a bit harsh on our Big Business friends. If so, it is to counter-balance the fawning treatment they often receive. I suspect that new investors may get a misleading idea that they have to be like these people in order to succeed. Investors may even get put off because they know they are not Big Business types.

Big Business people have great skills and flaws, as do we all. An honest look at these investors can make us look at ourselves and see if our behaviour is the same or different. Some features of a Big Business personality are:

- Energy, concentration and decisiveness.

- Competition with peers, family and themselves.

- Vision of future opportunities.

- Analysis of what they need to know.

- They sacrifice relationships if necessary.

- Highly pragmatic morals.

- Success symbols.

- Resilience in hard times. They can start again.

Chapter Two
Intellectuals

There is a myth about Intellectuals that they are smart. It is not always true. An Intellectual is simply someone with an independent and analytical mind. How much they store in that mind is another matter.

Ideally, Intellectuals will see a vision of the future like a Big Business person, including the long-term changes that affect society and business. But they will also focus on the details that fascinate them, sometimes to an extreme. This may lead to original ideas, but not necessarily. An Intellectual may simply be fascinated by a line of thought that many others have followed before. That is not a bad thing and it can be financially rewarding.

The mental activity of an Intellectual usually extends to the moral implications of what they do and believe. An Intellectual will therefore readily adapt to traditions in which moral qualities of honesty, integrity and self-sacrifice are required, like government service. These qualities are, in a sense, their own reward.

Some Intellectuals will find Big Business types to be distasteful. They may see the moral short cuts that the Big Business person has made, not their drive, energy or enthusiasm. This can give the Intellectual a perverse disdain for the market and all investment. The word "business" may even be repellent. They will say things like "I am terrible at looking after my finances", and laugh. Intellectuals may prefer a form of genteel poverty. It is enough that they did not prostitute their minds to filthy commerce.

If an Intellectual takes a serious interest in investing, they are most likely to throw themselves into it. Investing can become an intellectual pursuit for its own sake. In that case, the Intellectual will favour investments that they understand. It means researching many details and problems as possible. No one is better at doing this from nothing than the Intellectual.

Intellectuals tend to be careerists, but they are rarely found at the top of a company hierarchy. They are most likely to be mid-level managers or found in one of the professions like medicine, science, engineering or teaching. They can also make police detectives and military strategists.

Some Intellectuals may make their career out of selling their research and professional services to other investors. They may advise on highly complex products as well, such as derivatives. These advisers will be qualified, which at least impresses other Intellectuals.

Relationships

Intellectuals are known to seek out other like-minded people as collaborators or peers. At a superficial level they may be impressed by qualifications and titles. More importantly, Intellectuals need to discuss their thoughts with someone they respect, who shares the same interests or can give them the most interesting feedback. This is the origin of many professional societies. Membership, particularly if it is exclusive, may be attractive Intellectuals may like. However, once an Intellectual is sure of an investment they will act with independence. It will not bother them what anyone else thinks after their decision is made.

A tendency for the Intellectual to do what they think is right has a downside: They may sacrifice their existing relationships in order to get their career and social position. Intellectuals are prepared to spend years in training and wait decades for advancement before they reach their goal. It may be a senior rank, a professorship or public recognition of their role as an artist or author. This dedication may come at the expense of what their spouse or family may want. Some of the more impatient

Intellectuals will move for the training opportunities and earlier promotion, but rarely for just the money. This too can mean they leave behind old friends, but forces their family to do the same.

On the other hand, if the ambitions of the Intellectual are thwarted it may be a boost to their relationships. Intellectuals who are denied the opportunity to research and explore their ideas may contribute more to their family and community as a result.

Success

The Intellectual's motives may not be financial. They can be rewarded by their role, the freedom to think, or having the right budget, tools and assistants. You are more likely to see a rich Intellectual setting up their own backyard research institute or independent charity than buying a private jet.

Intellectuals may seek out symbols of achievement that are often non-financial in nature. For example, Intellectuals may value being called doctor or professor and put their qualifications on the wall. Published papers and prizes are just as important. Or a series of patents, whether or not any money is made from them. Intellectuals need to succeed on their own terms. Their idea of success may make no sense to anyone but them.

An Intellectual's style tends to mean that a capital base is built up slowly over many years, even if some short term opportunities are missed. Slow growth may also be favoured if the Intellectual moves around the country or is focused too much on their career. They will simply not have the time or spare intellectual capacity to focus on investment. But any investments that they do have may be in the form of cash or shares rather than residential property to allow for their mobile lifestyle.

The result may be a modest capital base, but the Intellectual may still have succeeded. *Financial success does not mean making huge amounts of cash, but as much money as you want to make.* An Intellectual with modest financial ambitions and a small amount of capital at the end would be a success. This realisation may prompt some Intellectuals to select a strategy that is right for them (see later chapters).

Failure

Financial failure rarely happens for an Intellectual because they set their standards so low. But if the Intellectual concentrates on investment then failure can occur because they do so too much. Other personalities might learn what they need to learn in order to make a return. Not the Intellectual. They will learn what interests them first, even if they go beyond what research is needed.

Time-wasting and over-analysis is a major issue for the Intellectual. They may spend so much time on research that they do not make enough money to meet whatever financial goals they have. Or they collect so much information that they cannot think it through properly. Confusion and poor decision-making may be the result.

Another reason that an Intellectual who invests does not meet their financial goals is concern about the law or good taste. Investment products that could be tax efficient are unlikely to appeal if there is a chance that the tax authorities could rule against them. Intellectuals may see the likelihood of a tax inspection and prosecution more clearly than a Big Business type who is focused on their tax bill.

If Intellectuals are community-spirited, then the health consequences of tobacco may be too great for them to invest in good conscience. Or if they are pacifists, then businesses like armaments or uranium mining could offend their inner code too much to take part. Strictly speaking, this reluctance is not failure, but it does mean that some opportunities will be missed.

A clearer source of financial failure are investments that are made after much research, but still lose money. This may simply be due to factors outside the knowledge or control of the investor. But if the failure was due to inadequate research or poor judgement then the results can be devastating. For the Intellectual it may mean that their mental ability was inadequate. This knowledge may affect their self esteem and how they see their position in society.

Failed investments and losses are so shameful that the Intellectual may take drastic action. They may go into self-denial and avoid admitting their mistakes. Family and friends may never know that the Intellectual has lost money unless they are bankrupted. Or the Intellectual may invent reasons for their own errors. Unfortunately, either approach may mean that the Intellectual does not confront their own mistakes or learn from them. In contrast, the Big Business personality may not care about the failure so much as making sure it does not happen again. It is just a step toward their next attempt at making money. That is not true for the Intellectual. They take their losses personally.

Summary

Some features of the Intellectual are:

- Independent thought and the confidence to follow their own judgement against the wishes of others.

- Vision in detail, which is an ability to see the overall trends as well as the facts that support them.
- Analysis or a greater depth of reasoning compared to the other investment personalities.

- Too much analysis, so may get bogged down in the details.

- Peer network.

- Moral outlook or a tendency to stand apart and see moral consequences of their actions.

- Career focused, so will sacrifice family and friends to promote their own career objectives.

- Non-financial symbols of success.

- Denial or a tendency to ignore failure and invent reasons that obscures their role in it.

Chapter Three
Small Business

Everyone knows the Small Business personality. They farm and trade the surplus, sell goods of every description in a shop and provide skilled services, including law, accountancy, construction and design. They may also lead a specialist division within a conglomerate or a regulator and run it like their own little country. Together, Small Business personalities employ most of the people in a nation.

It will not be a surprise that many Small Business people are shrewd. By this I mean that they conduct focused research and find out what they need to know. They also have practical judgement, honed by experience. It gives them the instincts for when to act or stay still.

Small Business owners have a stake in the moral conduct of the community. Theft in particular is of concern and they are outraged by insider trading. This is where investors trade using company information that is not public, which would affect the share price if it were known. In fact, some Small Business owners may feel cheated. They secretly would like to have used the inside information too. So it must be immoral if someone else got there first. Those who work as regulators miss out as well. A few may even come to dislike those Big Business types who beat the system and grow rich.

Small Business personalities tend to support law-and-order politicians. But their moral code is less rigid than the Intellectual. The Small Business person may be too close to financial disaster to be so proud. They can happily make a large profit on a deal even if the bargaining behaviour of a few gets a little too close to deceit. Naturally it is in their interests to treat their regular customers well if they want to be in business for any length of time. But otherwise they are there to make money without regret.

As a result, a Small Business personality may also be more comfortable than an Intellectual with investments like tobacco or uranium.

Another key feature of the successful Small Business person is their caution. This can be expressed as the need to keep a capital buffer (if they have that option). The buffer is a sum of money stored away for emergencies and updated as required. It may also take the form of inventory or assets and is popular in countries where folk don't trust the local currency, banks or the government. Either way, a capital buffer can mean that the Small Business person will survive a crisis. In contrast, a Big Business person is more likely to invest everything they have, despite the risk of doing so.

Some Small Business people develop bigger ambitions. They grow their business well beyond its' small operations, but further expansion can put their buffer at risk. The Small Business person will also have to work through others and be more selective about when and how they are involved. They must resist the temptation to micro-manage the details of their business when they should be steering it. A Small Business person could find this quite frustrating. They may also be frustrated at how long it takes a large organisation to respond to new conditions, when they were used to quick action. In other words, the skills that suit a Small Business person may be less useful if their business expands too much.

Some good news is that Small Business people can apply their business skills to investing. For example, they may develop expertise in a particular field or for a range of related companies. They may understand the markets, competitors, suppliers and customers of those companies better than most. It can also give them a view of the credit worthiness or financial strength of the companies in which they invest. So Small Business people can swoop on a bargain or make a tactical exit from an investment. This can be a competitive advantage over other investors. It is also not limited by growth in the size of their capital base.

Small Business people will invest in those products that they understand well. Cash investments like term deposits are an obvious choice. Likewise, property funds are based on 'bricks and mortar' and are something they can see and readily grasp. Small Business people are probably less attracted to new products with which they are unfamiliar, like hybrids or derivatives. They may also avoid international investments if they are unfamiliar with those foreign markets. An exception is when those investments relate to businesses in which they are experienced.

Relationships

A feature of Small Business people is their networking ability. They keep on good terms with their suppliers and customers. This is because people keep coming back to a business person that they like. Good relationships are also a source of useful information. Small Business people may learn what is about to happen in the economy or even what their competitors are doing. It is commercial intelligence that can help them to predict change and survive.

Small Business relationships may involve an element of calculation, like those of the Big Business person, but they never lose the knowledge that their business could fail. Small Business types therefore don't just need good relations with suppliers and customers. They also need a support network of family and friends. These are their next backers should they need to start again. Plus Small Business types also intend to stay in their community and often contribute to charities, sports clubs and other local organisations. It gives them a natural incentive to continue networking. It follows that

Small Business people tend to keep good relations with their network unless they are really reckless.

Success

If a Small Business owner succeeds as an investor (or in business), then they are likely to use a lower percentage of their money for big flashy purchases than a Big Business type. Otherwise it would consume money that they want to use for expansion. The Small Business owner remembers the last economic boom was followed by a downturn, so plans ahead. In fact, they add to their capital buffer to offset any future losses.

In addition, Small Business people will have family needs that take up part of their surplus. This is a side-effect of maintaining a network of family and friends. The Small Business person may feel obligated to help out family members or invest within their circle. Or they may simply be humble in their own ambitions. A happy family and a high standing in their community can satisfy many. But if they are really a Big Business type inside, then financial success could be the start of a new career. It may also signal the point at which they begin to let go of old relationships to make ones that are more useful.

Failure

If a Small Business personality fails at an investment then their capital buffer should ensure it is not fatal. At worst, their relationship network should also remain intact and this, together with their experience, ought to let them rebuild.

The Small Business person may feel less shame from financial loss than an Intellectual. Like the Big Business person, they may simply accept that failure and losses can happen when you are in business. Their social standing may not be too harmed either. Their like-minded friends and family may have the same outlook on investment. They are therefore not shocked if the Small Business type suffers a loss and could well be sympathetic.

If the Small Business personality has one horror it is being forced to work for someone else. This is what fear of failure really means for them. It may even cause them to keep a larger buffer and so restrict their investments. A Small Business person may therefore also take longer to rebound from a loss than would a Big Business type. A negative experience may make them even more cautious. If they were to blame they will acknowledge it. But that knowledge may be a brake on future action until they are confident they will not repeat their mistakes.

Summary

Some features of Small Business people are:

- Business experience that gives them sound instincts.

- Business network of suppliers and customers and skills in managing these relationships.

- Commercial intelligence gained by seeking out relevant information from customers and suppliers.

- Analysis of what is necessary.

- Decisive, so will swiftly respond to new conditions.

- Cautious about spending money. They may take time to make major business decisions if it is outside of their experience.

- Capital buffer or money that is put aside in case of financial emergency.
- Pragmatic morals, so may overlook extreme moral

objections to make money.

- Symbols of financial success extend to the needs of their family and community.

- Rebounds from failure with the assistance of their network.

Chapter Four
Team Players

The Team Player is the most popular of the personalities discussed in this book. They are found working on farms, in factories, shops, offices and many other jobs in government and business. Unfortunately, as Team Players are found so often in the labour market they can be the least paid.

Team Players are helpful and like to know where they stand. They are also good at working for a common cause, so enjoy competition as part of a group. To this end, they will follow the decisions of management or the team. It is behaviour that is consistent with a village environment where the community needed to work together to survive.

A feature of the Team Player is their level of comfort in a group. A Team Player is happy for anyone at a meeting to do a task provided it gets done. In contrast, an Intellectual would sit there and secretly hope to be asked to do it because of their skills. A Big Business personality would then choose someone and take the credit for their work. A Small Business personality, meanwhile, would have left the meeting to get started.

Do not expect Team Players to act independently or against their group. For example, they will follow the law even if they don't like it. Many Team Players find security in numbers and being part of the law-abiding crowd. To be independent and outside the law is to be open to criticism or exclusion.

When Team Players invest, they tend to win when everyone does. Or they exit the market in large numbers. Booms and panics are good signs that the Team Players are running. They will have a competitive advantage if they are quick enough to sense the market mood and act with it. The most successful Team Players may even act just ahead of the crowd. Many day traders, brokers and even successful long term investors seem to be Team Players or at least lean toward this personality type.

Team Players may simplify the investment process through the use of wise sayings or slogans. This might start out as "it is not what you know, but who you know". Then they might decide that "everything is risky", which is true enough, but use it to ignore the risk. With more experience, the Team Player could claim to "search for the yield", which is a way of ignoring high stock prices if they are expected to grow. I expect that there are many other examples. The problem is that slogans may just be laziness.

Relationships

A Team Player's network of friends and family is a source of strength. They are willing to listen and can be excellent at combining useful information from different sources. Indeed, many minds can be better than one, a view that loner Intellectuals may not grasp. But the value of this information is only as good as the sources. A Team Player's friends may all hold the same view, but it could still be wrong. If the Team Player lacks independent judgement they could be misled. Or they may buy into investments that they and their friends understand well, like cash deposits or property, but miss out entirely on those they do not.

Team Players are a joy to have as clients if you are an investment adviser. They will want to enter the market like all their friends and do not ask too many difficult questions. The hard part is to get them in the door because they are just as likely to trust what was written in the newspaper. Free seminars and lucky door prizes may work to bring them in. Give the crowd some slogans and ask them to hold up their hands if they all agree. Then watch the cash flow in. The downside is that some Team

Players have less money to invest. But the adviser who can get referrals to all their friends is made.

Perhaps the best approach for an adviser is to become the leader in the relationship. From the time when Team Players stumble and stammer about what they want, the adviser knows what is best and does not deviate from it. Team Players can be infected by the enthusiasm of others. Fraudsters know it too.

Success

When Team Players succeed financially they tend to spend the capital, not save or reinvest it. The Team Player's motive may be the same as Small Business people: they know that downturns may come. Here the effect is different because Team Players spend their money or share it with friends while it lasts. The Team Player's generosity may mean that they have less to reinvest and no capital buffer for hard times. But then a buffer is not needed if you have a steady job and lots of friends.

I have noticed that young Team Players buy superficial items like clothes, music and electronics. They spend like the flashier Big Business types, but the purchases are symbols of belonging not financial success. These youths want to be different like all their friends. The young Team Player may also lack the experience to see that economies grow in cycles and that hard times will follow the good.

Failure

If Team Players' investments fail, you can be sure that they will lose more than they can afford. It may then come as a surprise that the flashy, trendy items they bought are now worth very little. If burnt badly, the Team Player may avoid the market for years, missing a lot of bargains. Those who are scarred may finally create a capital buffer.

Some Team Players are inclined to believe there is a worldwide conspiracy by big business. Their talent for slogans may now come into play again: "The money has gone somewhere" and "Some benefit while others miss out". It does not help that Big Business personalities continue to celebrate. It seems some people sold before the slump occurred, but most of those who didn't were Team Players.

Financial failure will not hurt Team Players socially as all their friends are hurt too. Then they get together and blame others outside their group. Banks, brokers, advisers and anyone else who did exactly as they were asked to do will be a target. Dishonest parties are a better target.

The anger of Team Players as a group may be so great that governments respond with more laws and regulations. It is all that the politicians can do. They cannot make us better investors than we really are. Governments also have a tendency to make laws, but not give regulators enough money to do their job. It is easy to increase jail terms and fines, but costly to police the law. Or put another way, the first solution should be to use the laws that already exist.

The trouble with more law changes is that they can create a form of *moral hazard*. In this case, I mean that the law is used to give investors a false sense of security. So they continue to invest as before. Yet if the law has not changed how companies behave then the same problems will occur again and again.

It is simple for governments to avoid moral hazard: just do nothing and ignore the Team Players if they dare. It means that companies and investors are allowed to fail, so it forces everyone to take more responsibility. This is a truly wonderful idea, unless it is you who cannot pay your mortgage or feed your family. The social costs are simply to great to do nothing. So a balance is needed between moral hazard and the freedom to fail. It is a compromise to which I return in part four.

Summary

Some features of a Team Player are:

- Team work, so will co-operate with others to meet common goals.

- Good with relationships and have a genuine interest in others and helping them.

- Network of friends who are a source of information and support in time of crisis.

- Slogans may be used to help make decisions.

- Sensitive to market sentiment, so may detect the mood of the crowd and can exploit it.

- Little or no capital buffer. They may be too generous (to themselves or others) and not keep enough money aside for emergencies.

- Symbols of belonging.

- Group approach to finding fault for failure.

Chapter Five
Risk Tolerance

This chapter is about investment risk, but it is also about how you respond to it. That response is a feature of your personality and should affect what investment strategy you eventually choose. So it is important to understand something about risk and risk tolerance first.

Risk is simply what could happen in the future, good or bad. Going deeper, risk is a combination of the *likelihood* of an event happening and the *impact* if it does. It doesn't need to be much more complicated than that for the individual investor. It is though about intuition and opinion as much as hard facts. This makes risk assessment something that everyone can try.

Your response to risk, whether you embrace or control it, is a matter of your *risk tolerance*. It represents your overall level of liking for risk. It is based on your personality.

Risk

Every investment has risks, but we are only concerned with what is possible. Mice could eat all the wheat in a district, but it is not really going to happen as long as the farmers close their barn doors or hire more cats. In other words, we consider realistic outcomes when thinking about risks.

History is a major guide to risk. Repeated incidents of past pest damage can show what the cost of future damage could become. The frequency of that damage can indicate the likelihood of recurrence. History is not a fool-proof guide as the drivers for risk can change. But the market may assume that the historical risk will continue until informed otherwise.

The market is a moody place and may put more weight on one or two risks rather than the overall risk.

The market may therefore pay extra for an investment if it is believed that there is *upside risk of gain* to come. That is, the risk assessment favours profits, income and/or capital gains. On the other hand, if the market believes there is more *downside risk of loss*, it may reduce the price of an investment.[1]

The scale of the market response may increase in proportion to the risks. For example, there are risks at every step of a mining venture that are reflected in the price demanded by the market:

- Initial exploration may not yield enough mineral ore to be worth mining or good finds may not be sustained.
- The ore could be too deep and uneconomic to extract.
- It may be an unusual chemical composition and too costly to refine.
- The miners could demand more money in compensation to their risk of injury or disease.
- Capital may be wasted on superior expertise, surveys and mining technology if there is not enough ore.

The result is that investors often expect a large discount or reduction applied to the cost of shares when the company raises money. Investors stand to lose their shares if the venture collapses, but the payoff can be truly huge if the venture succeeds and the market's overall view of the risks reverses.

Risk Advice

There are probably two schools when it comes to risk advice: those who think too much about what can

---

1 I have seen inflation described as 'upside risk'. A better way to put it might be that the upside risk of economic growth can lead to the downside risk of inflation. It shows that risks may not be isolated.

go right and the rest who worry too much. Seeing either adviser can be a good idea actually, but investors need to pick the difference between impartial advice and a sales pitch.

Investment advisers are paid to invest money on behalf of their clients. They rank among those who see more of the upside risks than the downside. They like to focus on the risk of good profits and large share price gains. After all, they get paid if you invest, so may prefer to be encouraging about what can go right.

On the other hand, advisers who focus mainly on the downside risks would probably discourage too many investors. This kind of adviser is unlikely to survive by seeing private clients, so tend to work for companies. Naturally, it is in their interest to insert doubt and fear into the minds of these clients. The company will then need to pay someone (like, say, a risk adviser) to assess what can go wrong and make sure it does not happen.

Risk Tolerance

I have tried to look at risk in a simple way, but more questions need to be asked. Risk is high compared to what? Or low compared to what? As an investor you need to form a view about how risky an investment could be. But there is no ruler with risk stamped on it. Each investor must therefore form an overall view of risk, including the impacts and likelihoods of different outcomes. This view is a product of your *individual liking for risk or risk tolerance*.

For example, the more an investor is risk tolerant, the more they will see the upside potential and ignore or downplay the downside. If the impact of loss is clear, then the tolerant investor will mostly downplay the likelihood of failure. They may not even consider it. A more cautious investor though will do the opposite. They highlight the risks in their own mind and may avoid the most risky investments.

Furthermore, risk tolerance is influenced by your investment personality. Big Business types, Intellectuals, Small Business types and Team Players may view risk information differently. Their reactions are influenced by many factors, including how they research information, their relationships, as well as how they respond to financial success and failure. It therefore pays to understand how the investment personality is related to risk tolerance (see below). It may help you to understand your own tendencies as an investor. This includes the sort of risk advice you are likely to prefer at different times and why it is not a good idea to accept it without thinking.

Before I go any further, there is an exception to risk tolerance that must be mentioned: problem gambling. It is an addictive illness that may potentially affect investors too. The warning signs are listed in appendix one at the back of this book.

Big Business People

It is fair to say that the Big Business personality is one of the most comfortable with risk. They will consider it as much as they feel they need to. Often they will focus on the impacts were an investment to go badly, like the most they could lose. If they can accept this loss then the Big Business person may be far less concerned with the likelihood that it will happen. Indeed, Big Business types have a tendency to see every risk as so remote as not to be worth worrying about. They have a point: more companies would collapse more often if the likelihood was higher. It is also a practical view because the impacts may be calculated, whereas the likelihoods can be anyone's guess. Big Business types have much more to do than sit and worry about chance. They have a grand plan and are itching to get started.

Big Business people may make great investment

advisers. They see the limited downside, but love the upside. Some may let their clients overlook the likelihood of failure until their cheque is signed. Other Big Business people also are willing to hire advisers to tell them about the best opportunities. They are prepared to pay for the right advice and will even seek out information about the downside risks. Or they will do enough of their own research and then make a quick decision. It is not that the Big Business people ignore risk. They simply deal with it and move on.

A pragmatic take on life allows the Big Business personality to accept risks without undue concern for the consequences. Risk does not eat away at them with worry or sleepless nights. Actually, an element of risk may make the whole venture all that more exciting. Big Business people are therefore likely to be attracted to riskier products like derivatives and want to find out more about them. Or they may put a high proportion of their capital in large investments that concentrates their risk.

If the situation changes and the downside risks become clearer, then Big Business types will be equally decisive in quitting their position. They tend not to be sentimental about a money-making scheme. In other words, they can quickly become risk intolerant and exit.

Intellectuals

Intellectuals are much more likely to spend time worrying about risk. This is not the same as fearing risk itself, but rather it is fear that they have not understood the risks of an investment well enough. There may be too many other risks that they have not thought of either. These thoughts can weigh down the Intellectual and make them too cautious or risk-adverse.

Intellectuals respond to risk by more research. A careful and methodical examination of the past could be worthwhile in case history repeats itself. In this way,

Intellectuals can develop a detailed understanding of risk. Their research can in fact become a competitive advantage, provided they do not spend all their time on it. The point will come when Intellectuals have to stop the research and make a decision. But if an Intellectual is comfortable with their research then they will approach investment without fear. Indeed, Intellectuals can be highly risk tolerant if they think they understand the risks.

Small Business People

The Small Business types understand business risk only too well. They have the commercial experience and instincts which make an assessment of likelihood and impact easy, even if they do not put it in those terms. As a result, Small Business types should have a better understanding of risk impacts and likelihood than the rest of the market. This is a competitive advantage. However, the Small Business person is far more intolerant of risk if the investment is outside of their experience.

What sets the Small Business person apart is their natural risk management outlook, often expressed as a capital buffer. Other investors may create a buffer, but this personality does so instinctively. The size of the buffer is a product of their risk tolerance. A smaller buffer may be required for investments in areas where they have expertise and so a higher tolerance for risk. A larger buffer will therefore be required for investments in areas outside of their experience.

Team Players

Successful Team Players sense what the rest of the market is up to better than anyone else. They understand market sentiment and maybe what is driving it. This is their safety net. It is also very large and often reliable. It makes Team Players extremely tolerant of risk. In fact, they may make no risk assessment at all. It is enough that all their friends and colleagues tell them a good deal is to be had for them to invest.

The problem with this approach is that the Team Player's safety net can vanish. The market mood can change and a boom turn into a crash. If Team Players have not acted fast enough then they will quickly become the least risk tolerant of the investors. This does not mean that their analysis has become any better. Instead they panic and run with the rest.

Summary

It should be clear by now that risk is the chance than an investment will do good or bad and by how much. How you see risk and you liking for it, or risk tolerance, is linked to your investment personality. If I were to rank everyone from the highest to the lowest risk tolerance, I would say the rough order is as follows:

- *Highest Risk Tolerance*: The Team Player (in boom-mode) who trusts others, sees the upside and may over-buy.

- *2nd Highest Risk Tolerance*: Big Business types (risk is unclear) who research impacts and assumes that the downside likelihood is low.

- *3rd Highest Risk Tolerance:* The Intellectual (well-researched) and Small Business (experienced) who trust their own judgement and knowledge.
- *3rd Lowest Risk Tolerance:* The Intellectual (poorly researched) and Small Business (inexperienced) who do not trust their own judgement and knowledge.

- *2nd Lowest Risk Tolerance:* Big Business types (risk is clear) who sell quickly if circumstances change and the downside risk is bigger than expected.

- *Lowest risk tolerance:* The Team Player (in panic mode) who trusts others, sees the downside and may over-sell.

These rankings can be good or bad news depending on what you think is your risk tolerance level. Take some time now to review your investment personality traits for investment and your risk tolerance. Together these form the basis of your investment style.

Chapter Six
Should I Change?

By now you have had a chance to think about which of the personalities fits you best. Perhaps it is so clear that you could skip this chapter. But for most people, a chance for reflection is probably needed. It is time to take stock of the last five chapters and if you are comfortable with what you found. That is what this chapter is for: a pause for reflection before deciding what to do next.

Think about your reaction to the previous chapters. If one personality and risk tolerance stood out, then that is probably what is right for you. I suggest you go with your gut feeling rather than some detailed analysis. Often our first impression is the most important.

On the other hand, do you prefer to remember the negative stuff? You may choose to focus on criticism rather than praise. Or did you skim over your faults a little too easily? You may not have a balanced view and so be unsure about your investment personality or risk tolerance. If necessary, go back and read some chapters again.

Your assessment may not end even if you have a clear understanding of your personality and risk tolerance. Do you accept yourself as you are or try to change? I will start to answer this question in this chapter.

Big Business Fetish

Some people seem to believe that the only way to be successful financially is to act like a Big Business person. I mean the chief executive officers and wealthy investors who are covered in newspaper articles, books, on radio and television programs. They get treated with respect and sometimes with sucking noises. It is hard to avoid the impression that there is something so good about them that they deserved to become rich. But these Big Business types are always a minority. If everyone could change to become like them then the world would be even more competitive than it is already.

I am not going to try and persuade you to become a Big Business personality if you are different. This false view could lead you to choose a strategy that is wrong for you. The danger is that you may copy the behaviour and risk tolerance of someone you envy, but not truly absorb their personality. You may want their wealth, but not be prepared to work their hours, lose your family and friends to achieve it or die from a stress at forty. Or you may not truly be willing to lose everything like a Big Business person. In my opinion, *it is better to improve who you are as an investor than try to be someone you are not.*

Combinations

Once the Big Business fetish is put aside, some folk may be forced to look more closely at themselves. It is possible that you act like different personalities in different circumstances. For example, you may act like a Small Business personality when dealing with investments you know very well. But the rest of the time you might act like a Team Player who relies on friends or friendly experts. Or you might be an Intellectual who loves research, but not about financial data. You may instead act like a Team Player and invest with the crowd. Or act like a Big Business personality and learn only enough to invest. These kind of differences can lead to questions about which is your real personality and risk tolerance. It may lead to confusion about which path to take.

The kind of splits I mention above are probably more common than many realise. It could be what works for you, but it may also be confusing. You may wonder how far you can change what you have and bring your investment behaviour, underlying personality and risk tolerance into better alignment. It could make you more confidant as an investor and about the strategy that you choose. I think that your genetics, upbringing and life circumstances are relevant to the answer.

Genetics

Children develop their personalities at a very early stage as parents will know. Anecdotal evidence for this view is found in an old saying, 'Show me the boy when he is five and I will show you the man.' This early development may be due to genetics. So much is now linked to our DNA that I would not be surprised if personality and risk tolerance are too.

Some genetic effects are known to be shared by many, like the risk tolerant brains of teenagers. They may understand the risks of an activity, such as mountain climbing, but want to do it anyway. Their excitement may therefore override any concerns. Some people could react in the same way to exciting investments that are too good to miss.

More subtle differences may exist between adults. In fact, you could have a genetic leaning towards risk-taking behaviour that finds expression in your brain. If so, changes to your personality and risk tolerance are unlikely to happen no matter what you do. But there are some exceptions to consider: upbringing and life restrictions.

Upbringing

It is uncontroversial to say that our youth is a time when we learn ethics or moral values. It will affect how we behave and invest. The views of our parents, religious leaders and the general community will therefore have a powerful influence. The economic environment is important too. For example, an investor who grows up in a stable environment with enough to eat may be more tolerant of risk than one who did not. These experiences combine with our personality to form our risk tolerance (unless it was genetics all along).

For many, our upbringing will stay with us and is consistent with our underlying personality. But if there is a clash in any way it may come out as a teenage rebellion. Teens may then find mentors whose views better suit their personality. The effects of our upbringing can therefore be modified to some extent at an early stage.

In addition, an environmental change could alter how we behave. For example, imagine a young Team Player from a small, stable community who moves to the city in her late teens. She enters a stockbroking firm and her eyes are opened to a totally different world. Maybe she finds a rich mentor and her outlook to making money and taking risk changes. She gains new friends who share similar views. Eventually she is investing like them too. In doing so, her risk tolerance changes, even if it clashes with how she was brought up. It may even clash with her underlying personality.

A more complicated scenario involves chief executive officers and senior executives who have 'grown up' within an organisation. They changed along the way, but not completely. Some may operate with a kind of split personality: what they were taught at home and what they have become in order to survive at work. A business leader can therefore host a team celebration at their house then fire the lot a few weeks later. It is like they have two sets of values that sit side-by-side in their brain. This difference can also come out in how they approach risk in private investment and at work.

The result is that risk tolerance is based on genetics and personality, but is also modified by our upbringing. This can create a patchwork of influences over risk tolerance and lead to the combinations and confusion mentioned earlier. The trouble is that our formative years are just that: they form how we think and behave. So unless you are still quite young it may be difficult to resolve a clash of personality and risk tolerance by a fundamental change. It is better to improve what you have.

Restrictions

I should mention another important influence over risk tolerance: restrictions caused by life circumstances. But these restrictions are more of a mask over our risk tolerance, not a fundamental change. So if the restrictions are lifted then our risk tolerance will again be revealed.

For example, someone who has children should find that these little ones become central to their life. They are also expensive. So the parent will have less money to invest and more concern about the effects of failure on their family. But this restriction on their risk tolerance may weaken if they win a lottery or the kids finally leave home. Then their natural risk tolerance may be revealed.

Older investors too may be restricted by their experience of economic recessions. They know better than most that the warm days of summer will cease. But then some people at the very end of their lives act in surprising ways. They might wonder, 'What have I got to lose?' and go skydiving, or make some short-term speculative investments just for fun. It could be that the restrictions on their risk tolerance have relaxed to reveal the real risk-taker.

Restrictions on risk tolerance are another source of a clash between personality and risk tolerance. Often the restrictions cannot be resolved in the short term. Instead, investors need to work with them and improve what they have.

A Solution

If your investment personality and risk tolerance seem to clash, whatever the cause of genes, upbringing or life restrictions, it is not the end. The good news is that you should still be able to improve. A solution is to look more closely at your goals, strengths and weaknesses. That is what part two of this book is about. It may show that there is less of a clash than you feared or at least how to improve what you have.

Summary

Investment style is a combination of your investment personality and risk tolerance. The development of risk tolerance has strong influences from genetics and upbringing, though it may be restricted for a time by other factors like family commitments or experience. The combined effect could be a clash between your risk tolerance and your underlying personality. This can cause confusion.

There is little to be gained by idolising those rich investors who have a different investment style. It may even be harmful to try and change to become like them. Instead it is better to improve what you have, which is what the next chapters are about. Knowledge of your goals, strengths and weaknesses can be used for improvement and potentially bring your personality and risk tolerance into better alignment.

PART TWO
Style Improvements

How to Use Part Two

Part two builds on the self-knowledge that you have of your personality and risk tolerance. The idea is to find the goals, strengths and weaknesses that best fit who you are and your life circumstances. What follows is a series of choices in which you make the most of your investment style. Some people will want to skip straight to choosing an investment strategy (see part three). But there is a risk of underperformance because they do not apply their style to its' full advantage.

The next chapter is about goals and has a dual-purpose: to identify what goals you have now and, if you like, create some more. This process may expose whether your existing goals truly suit your personality and risk tolerance. It may be that you need new goals instead. Or your risk tolerance may be restricted by circumstances, including legitimate goals, even though the result clashes with your personality. This chapter may help you to clarify how much you can realistically improve.

The chapters on strengths and weaknesses are about the behavioural tools for meeting or missing your goals. They are linked to your personality and risk tolerance too. However, strengths and weaknesses are not limited to one particular personality, even though some may seem better suited to one or more of them. Partly this may be due to influences like upbringing.

Part two is basically a series of tips and tricks for improving your investment style. The funny thing is that most of this information turns out to be common sense. You might really know it already, but prefer not to think about it. I suggest you use your instinct: does a tip *feel* right? Does it feel right even if it is uncomfortable too?

Chapter Seven
Your Goals

The first step toward developing your investment style is to list your goals. This process is more than saying you want a big sock that is full of cash. What is it that you want to achieve in life and what is needed to fund it? It is important here to think about what you actually want deep down inside and that fits your personality and risk tolerance.

Be Specific

Be wary of anyone who wants you to be the best that you can be. The problem is that perfection is impossible to achieve. It is a great way though to set yourself up to fail. It could work well for those with low self-esteem who like to beat themselves up. For the rest of us, it pays to improve what we have. That means specific goals.

Here are some questions to ask yourself about what it is you want to achieve. I suggest you gauge their importance by how you feel about each goal. Don't think too much. Do you want to invest to:

- Have more spending money?
- Educate your children?
- Leave poverty?
- Build a stake to invest in a business?
- Pay off your home loan early?
- Buy your parents a home?
- Save for retirement?
- Help your family?
- Gain independence?
- Work on what really interests you?
- Have fun?
- Beat the market?

- Become an investment specialist?
- Impress your friends?
- Be a part of your country's development?
- Fund social, religious or environmental goals?

Some of these questions were probably still not specific enough. So another way to approach the same questions is to ask what is the minimum you would need to meet a goal. For example, how much money would you really need to leave your job and retire? How much money would it take to make you feel good if you went to a class reunion? How much does private education for your kids cost? And so forth.

If your goals still appear to be too open-ended, it may work to think about some investment benchmarks. A classic benchmark for investors is the interest rate on a cash deposit, or the average return on the stock market or a fund. These benchmarks should be exceeded if your efforts are to be worthwhile. An exception might be in the first few years when you give yourself permission to learn. Otherwise, you might be better to put your money in the bank or hand it over to an experienced and qualified fund manager.

Risk Tolerance Goals

Perhaps the section on goals was familiar to you. Goals have been written about by countless authors. Parents and schoolteachers can also get in on the act and push you to succeed in a way they think is right.

Risk tolerance goals are slightly different. They are linked to the discussion of risk tolerance in chapter five and what you recognised about yourself. We saw that risk tolerance is your liking for risk, a combination of the upside and downside risks, or what can go right and wrong. Your risk tolerance is internal guidance for the risks that you are prepared to take. *Risk tolerance goals are therefore what you aim to do in order to keep within your risk tolerance level.*

Here are some more questions:

- How much money would you be prepared to lose at once?
- What level of debt would keep you awake at night?
- How much money would you need to start again?
- Could you face family and friends if you lost money?
- Could you ask family and friends for a loan and for how much?
- What level of gains would make you feel confident/ nervous about an upturn in the market?
- What level of losses would make you feel confident/ nervous about a downturn in the market?
- What is the minimum level of gains that would make you relax and enjoy your wealth?
- What level of financial change would cause you to stop and reassess your goals?

These questions will be scary for some and tedious for the most risk tolerant. But the result should be that you end up with an extra list of goals for your own peace of mind. For example, you might aim to cap your losses at X figure, or re-evaluate your portfolio if the gains reach Y level. But it can still be difficult to know where to set your limits. Knowledge of your available capital can help.

How Much Have You Got to Invest?

It sounds simple: make a decision about how much money to invest to meet your goals. But how many people ever really do that? Maybe those who have a spreadsheet at home with all their income and expenses listed and graphed. The rest of us may spend what we have in our pockets at the time. Yet a clear-sighted understanding of what you can afford to put at risk in the market is important.

It may highlight what you are really prepared to lose. Use this insight to clarify your risk tolerance goals.

One way to begin is to ask yourself how much available capital do you have now? Don't answer by reference to your credit card limit or how much a bank would loan to you. Too many people have made this mistake, 'invested' in all sorts of goods and services, then discovered permanent debt. I am also not going to count the things you could sell, since I expect you want to keep them. For now, just consider what you know you have in cash investments. The answer will be zero for many. New investors would probably also not consider debt funding just yet (see chapter sixteen). So your available capital is probably any savings that you have or nothing.

Now add your income. What do you expect to earn this year? This is a starting point to find out how much of this income is available for investment. The spreadsheet gurus will already have subtracted all their expenses to leave net available income. Life is not quite that detailed for everyone, however. Plenty have their rent or mortgage repayments taken out of their salary and then they spend the rest. By the end of the week it is all gone. So it still might look like you have zero available income at first glance.

Another version of the same question is to ask how much of your salary would be left after your major bills are paid? This includes food, utilities like electricity and water, plus health insurance, school fees and so on. It may be easier to look at this over the period of a year. The result will be rough, but the estimate of your available capital is now your cash savings, if you have any, plus your potential available income before luxuries like entertainment are taken out. I am not saying that you would invest all of your available income. But it may show you that you have more options to invest than you thought.

Intellectuals may need to stop thinking of all the possible expenses and pick a high level figure. Big Business types do this automatically or even just pick the arbitrary figure, so they can move on. Small Business types will take a detailed approach like Intellectuals, but seem more likely to have this information at their finger tips. Team Players can pick their expenses like everyone else, though they may find it productive to do so as part of a group. It is quicker if their friends call out their ideas about expenses and the result will probably be the best guesstimate of all.

The value of knowing your available capital is to help you clarify you risk tolerance goals, particularly what you are prepared to lose. Unfortunately, there will be some who, after going through the exercise above, still do not have enough available capital to invest. One solution is to earn more, but that is clearly outside the scope of this book. However, you can at least learn while you earn. Your best plan at this stage may be simply to research the strategies outlined in part three of this book. Then when you do have enough capital you will also have more knowledge with which to invest.

A few will simply not be able to put money aside or keep their hands off their savings. You clearly will have no available capital. An investment adviser may be your best option and that's fine. They can set up a plan for you. But if you are able to resist raiding your savings, then why not become an investor? The next section is for those people who have the willpower, but need more idea about how to increase their available capital.

Increase Your Available Capital

In this section, I discuss some of the ways to increase what you have to invest (apart from earning more). Other books may cover these ideas too, so I have kept this part brief.

(a) Budgeting

It seems to be human nature to spend what you earn. The more you earn, the higher your expectations of standard of living may become, so the more you spend. But it doesn't have to be that way. A plan for how much you spend out of your income each week can help. By limiting your costs you may create a surplus. This can be saved or invested.

It is possible to learn to watch your spending. If you like collecting receipts and totting up your purchases then go for it. You may be surprised to see how much is spent on luxuries. These could be reduced without threat to your income or health. It sounds easy until you consider whether you want to give up your mobile phone in order to save money for investing. Many people will not, even though it is a luxury. Some will even invent reasons why a mobile is really is a necessity. They may need a savings plan instead.

(b) Savings plan

A savings plan is the agreement you make with yourself to put money aside. This money could come from a budget surplus, but here I mean that you save first and then spend. One way is to ask your bank to make an automatic deduction from your salary as it is paid into your account. The deduction may go into a special savings account or a fund. You are then free to spend what is left. This is a good approach if you tend to spend all you have, but can cope with less if necessary.

If you shop around, you may find a bank account that rewards you with additional interest for regular saving. You may not need a huge amount of capital at the beginning, just enough to buy a parcel of shares or other securities (though this will concentrate your risk). In this way, you can make investments bit-by-bit as you save enough to invest and steadily build your investments.

(c) Find a Mentor

If you know anyone with budgeting or saving skills, they may be worth approaching for advice. Some personalities do this as a matter of course. You cannot expect to learn everything from just one book, so ask others for advice and build up your own store of wisdom. Big Business people and Team Players are particularly good at it. Small Business types may do so within their own circle. Intellectuals may need more of a push.

Education

Use education to fill gaps in your knowledge about investing. It may help you realise what is achievable and so contribute to the creation of realistic goals. Here are some suggestions:

- Do an educational course (eg. accounting).
- Find a course in the education supplement of major newspapers.
- Join an investment club as other members could become mentors.
- Check out your local library for general investment books and club notices.
- Read the financial press regularly.
- Learn to use an internet search engine.
- Use the internet to find databases, research reports and specialist investment books.
- Explore a market exchange website to find company reports, financial ratios and charts.
- Check out different broker websites find analyst reports and guidance.

A word of warning about education: courses can be a trap if you just turn up. You risk wasting your money unless you are clear about what you want to get out of it. There is no point memorising a lot of information for an exam if it cannot be used later. It is better to withdraw or fail that course. Or at least focus on the interesting bits so you learn what you want. A bad sign is if you are motivated by grades or by adding qualifications to your resumé.

Timeframes

A goal is pointless without a timeframe in which to achieve it. Don't just pick an arbitrary date like next year. Try to fit a reasonable timeframe to your goals and your available capital. If this seems too hard, you might need to break the task down into mini-goals and shorter timeframes. Be honest with yourself, particularly if you are starting out. How long will it realistically take to achieve your goals with the money you have available? You may need to consider your likely needs in the next year or even the next five to ten years. The period is up to you and how far into the future you have set your goals.

Improve Your Alignment

Some investors, after reading part one of this book, might think their investment personality and risk tolerance clash. For example, they may have a high risk tolerance that does not seem to suit a cautious Intellectual. Or they have one risk tolerance at work and another for private investment. Or they may have a personality that favours risk-taking, but be frustrated by a risk tolerance that is constrained by family circumstances or limited available capital.

Thinking about your goals and risk tolerance goals may reveal what you really want. Or if you consider all your goals together, it may show which ones do not fit and can be cut. This is particularly important for people who have picked up false ideas about the sort of personality and risk tolerance that they need to be a successful investor. In fact, your real goals may be far more consistent with your personality than you realised, or point to what they really are. The next chapters on strengths and weaknesses will also supply further evidence.

In addition, the process of looking at your available capital and timeframes is a useful reality check. It can show you if your goals can really be achieved. It may be that these restrictions on your risk tolerance are the source of a clash with your personality. Your underlying risk tolerance may in fact be different and more consistent with your personality. If so, it could be useful to make a series of minor goals. For example, your new goals may involve budgeting, getting out of debt, building available capital, education along the way and then targeted investment as you build your wealth. This is an ongoing process that breaks your bigger investment goals into achievable chunks. It is also a path to realising your true risk tolerance.

Of course, I should not forget the slight chance that some find more available capital than they thought they had. These unusual people could adjust their goals and timeframes to become more ambitious. They may could afford to be more risk tolerant if it suits them.

Write it Down

Do you need to write your ideas so far? That is, write out your conclusions about your personality, risk tolerance, goals, risk tolerance goals, available capital and timeframes. Some books might recommend it as a way to add clarity and commitment. Then again, these authors may be people who just like that sort of thing. You may not. It is like going grocery shopping: some folk like a detailed written list, but others hate to be that structured. I'll leave it to you. Write down a summary and keep it somewhere safe if you think it will help. (Hey, chant your goals at the mirror each morning if it will do any good).

Summary

Investment goals may show what is really important in your life. It helps to be specific and a series of questions were provided to prompt answers. You could then cut goals that are incompatible with your overall direction. These goals may also reveal your real self. This is important if you have absorbed false ideas about the personality and risk tolerance you need to succeed.

Of course, a limitation is that amount of money and time that you have to invest. A basic process was given to find out about your available capital. This is a useful reality check for your goals, which may need to be revised. It may show that your risk tolerance is really just restricted by circumstances. It also points to a solution: create a series of smaller goals to build available capital, along with education on a path to investment. These goals can be integrated within a broader series of investment goals.

In the next two chapters we look at strengths and weaknesses. These are what you apply to meeting your goals or new goals. The way you approach them could also affect your success in choosing and applying an investment strategy.

Chapter Eight
Use Your Strengths

An assumption in this chapter is that people enjoy what they are good at doing. Each step, each success is a positive reinforcement of those strengths. So if we apply the strengths from our personality to investing, we will enjoy investing and want to do more of it. We should then try to improve our strengths. These improvements will be natural and absorbed more readily.

It is important to take some time to identify your strengths. You will probably already know some anyway, or got ideas from earlier chapters. I have made a list of what I think are some common strengths that successful investors may have. I have also included some ideas for how to develop these strengths and use them more often. Even if you do not agree with my list, it could inspire you look at what your real strengths are. Please avoid picking strengths that you think you *should* have. If this exercise is to have any value it is through honest self-analysis. You do not have to tell anyone.

Careful with Money

Are you good at budgeting? If you can limit your costs and save more, then you will obviously have more to invest. This is why people who spend money freely hate you. They waste their cash on items that lose value as soon as they step outside the shop. Meanwhile you build an investment portfolio and a better income.
Take another look at this skill. It addresses the risk that you will run out of cash. It also requires discipline to be careful with your money. Can you apply this talent more broadly? After all, it requires discipline to set buy and sell triggers, to watch the market and then act on them. Perhaps you might make a good trader if you can stand the stress (see chapter ten). You may be able to review

your portfolio, cut your losses and live for another day. You will still need to understand what you are buying, of course.

Of all the investment personalities, the Small Business type seems to be the best suited to a disciplined approach. They have to guard their capital buffer, watch their stock, customers and overheads. Successful Small Business people cannot afford to be sentimental about anything if they are to survive the economic cycle. Intellectuals will be disciplined too once they are certain of what they want. The Big Business personality can be frugal as well, if they need to be, until they decide that spending is worthwhile. I am not so sure that Team Players will be, unless their family and friends are too.

News Watcher

Do you enjoy reading the newspaper or watching the news on television or the internet? There is something addictive about finding out what is happening or how events at a distance can affect those closer to home. This curiosity and a liking for how events fit together can be a very useful strength. It can be used to address the risks from investing when information is scarce.

Does your news exposure extend to the business news? Some people, even though they want to invest, are a little shy of the business section in a newspaper. It is somehow too technical and the jargon can be confusing. True, it is like that for many people to start with, but do what you do with the rest of the news: filter out what is not of interest. You might think that you need to read and understand everything. But who really does that? Think of a process by which you gradually build up knowledge. Many financial papers include articles aimed at new players. Over a period of time you will read and absorb far more than you realise. And the more you know, the more interesting it may become.

You might start with business news items that deal with people. Actually, most news is about people in some way or another. Even numbers in the financial press can represent the behaviour of customers or the population at large. You may also develop a preference for the articles by particular journalists or news programs. They are set at your level of understanding. Over a period of time, you should figure out which experts know what they are talking about, whose predictions come true and those who just repeat what they have heard.

Consider how to extend your interest in the news. At a simple level, you may follow how the market responds to it. For example, a company may pay more of its profits to investors and share prices rise as a result. There will be many who want to exploit this news, so the question is how closely can you monitor the news and how quickly can you act on it? If not, is it still useful as a long term opportunity?

For example, a Team Player may figure out from reading many articles and talking with their friends that there is a relationship between interest rates and the exchange rate with country X. So it is possible to guess the effects of news about higher interest rates on a company that makes a lot of its profit from importing from that country. The Team Player can invest accordingly when interest rates are expected to change. They could be the best News Watchers.

Or the news may trigger actions based on experience. A Small Business person may know how higher interest rates will affect the key suppliers to an industry. So even though most investors in that industry are not concerned initially, the Small Business person is able to sell out before the cost of supplies go up and financial performance is harmed.

Does your interest and experience extend to international events? A succession of politicians, laws and regulations, free trade agreements, central bank intervention and other economic developments can drastically affect different economies. This in turn will affect companies which import from or export to those countries. You may be able to predict the effects back home and invest accordingly. Others can do this too, but the understanding of foreign countries varies. It may therefore pay to study the structures and economies in large foreign countries.

If you know a second language, preferably of a major trading partner, you may also benefit from hearing foreign news slightly quicker because you know the lingo. Even if you don't, opportunities can still arise after an initial market reaction has subsided. Investors may be more concerned with local news and so other information takes their attention. Investors who have developed their knowledge of foreign news over time, including which issues have the most effect, may then make successful investments.

Number Cruncher

Do you have an ability to read and understand numbers? Do you enjoy or even prefer maths to other subjects? It is very likely that you could cope with financial statements from companies, whereas other people will flinch at the thought. Just because you like numbers, don't forget there are many people out there who have been maths-phobic since high school. They cannot understand that equations are like music to those who can understand them. Investors who have an ability with maths may therefore have a competitive advantage.

Financial numbers (like earnings and profit) are useful because they are a means to summarise a gigantic range of information. Numbers therefore address the risk that you invest without knowing enough about a company. Unusual or unexpected numbers are then a trigger for further investigation.

One way to find out if you can cope is to obtain the financial statements of some sample funds or companies. These are typically available on the internet. Start with companies that have businesses which you find interesting or with which you have experience.

A short course in accounting could have you reading the financial statements of companies and comparing them. If the differences do not make sense, then other investors may have the same problem. It could be that one company is better managed, or it has engaged in what is politely called 'creative accounting'. There are laws against misrepresentation, but the auditors only sign off that the accounts are fair and reasonable (or similar words) for a reason. There is still room for differing interpretation of the law and accounting standards as well as company accounting policies. A Number Cruncher may form an opinion about whether the differences between companies are due to more than interpretation and avoid the suspicious firms.

The Small Business type will be drawn to those companies of which they have experience. They can become experts in a particular field or industry and quote the main figures and statistics of their favourites from memory. It may also mean that they can quickly detect odd figures or inconsistencies for investigation.

The Big Business type studies just enough to read a financial statement if they need to. If these people ever quote financial information, you can be sure it is what influenced their investment decision. They are unlikely be fascinated enough to want to become an expert. But at least they learn enough to understand the recommendations of their advisers, industry jargon and what they read in the financial press.

The Intellectual may read financial numbers, but as one factor in formulating a plan. The Intellectual will want to see how all this information fits together, what trends emerge or even how a company would fit into their portfolio. Numbers alone are unlikely to fascinate them.

The Team Player tends not to read numbers for fun unless it is truly their strength. The challenge for them is to come up with some rules that can be used to assess financial performance. Financial ratios are useful for this purpose (see appendix four for examples).

Big Picture Artist

As a child, did you think about the consequences of your actions more than most? Did you know that everyone would get into trouble if the class clown misbehaved? I don't mean that you were paranoid, but you were able to see beyond the immediate activity in front of you to the future. It is also a useful skill that can be applied to investing.

Financial information is often just a jumble. There is a risk of information overload so it is difficult to pick out what is relevant or missing. A Big Picture Artist can integrate information that does not seem to be related at all. What is important is easy enough to see in hindsight. The artist is someone who can see the connections between financial numbers, people, law, economics and so forth to form a view about an investment and act before everyone else. Details people think you are a flake, but you can make intuitive decisions that pay. This skill is particularly useful when the evidence is fragmented or incomplete.

Big Picture Artists look for patterns and trends in market behaviour or curious gaps. But it goes further than that. You are the scavengers of the investing world, finding all manner of interrelated information about strategy, management, culture, risks and so on. Then you put it all together, stand back and see where the trends and opportunities lie. These investors see the forest, not just the trees.

A major source of big picture information is the media, but you will have to piece it together over a long period of time. Other major sources are company reports, analyst presentations and announcements. These may contain information about how companies are run, their strengths and objectives. If you are not a numbers person, then don't force yourself to read all the accounts. You will go cross-eyed. Focus instead on the words and what is and isn't said. What does it mean for the company strategy? Does it point to any competitive advantage or disadvantage compared to their rivals?

I don't recommend going to the Annual General Meetings of most public companies. There are too many old people asking strange and irrelevant questions. These shareholders then eat an amazing number of sandwiches and go home for another year. You could send in specific, written questions to fill the gaps in your knowledge, but I suspect you will get a very general answer.

One way to find out if you have potential as a Big Picture Artist is to choose a stock or company with which you are familiar. Next, note everything you know about it: the products, the customer base as well as legal and economic issues that could affect it. Does it tell you anything about the prospects for that company? You may be surprised at how much you really know and have a strength on which you can build.

Among the personalities, a Big Business type will probably focus on what they like doing: setting the vision, energising and motivating the staff, identifying and attacking the competition, beating the market and seeing their pay packets rise faster than everyone else. But their intuition and ability to integrate enough different information into their vision is at the heart of their success. Intellectuals too make good Big Picture Artists provided they know when to stop looking and start doing. Small

Business types are Big Picture Artists on a smaller scale. They may look at the big picture, but for fewer investments. Team Players are the natural integrators of information, but may have difficulty with this strength due to a limited outlook. They may have skills they do not know about.

Match Maker

Do you like to imagine who of your friends could be suited romantically? It is probably stretching the point, but there are people who can do something like it for companies. They can imagine potential arrangements, such as where two company merge together to form one. Another example is where one company takes over or buys another, through trading shares on a market or directly with shareholders off-market. These arrangements and the legal fights that can lead up to them will often affect the share price of each company.

Match Makers are a type of specialist Big Picture Artist. They need to integrate a wide range of financial information, strategy, people and business environment issues into their thinking. Some Match Makers may even do this for a living as advisers.

Match Makers may ask a range of questions to find the *synergies* or benefits that would not be possible if the entities remained separate.

- What are the expansion prospects for an industry?
- Do any of the competitors have inherent advantages that favour organic growth?
- Is the ability of companies to raise dividends limited?
- Do business conditions, such as interest rates or market demand for shares, favour finding the money for takeovers?
- Is there a market trend for mergers and takeovers?
- Are mergers and takeovers fashionable amongst

directors?

- Does the financial media respond positively to mergers and takeovers?
- Could management improve the operation of the target?
- Could the management teams get along with each other if combined?
- Do the businesses have compatible cultures?
- How tolerant of mergers are the customers and regulators?
- Could the combined company act like a monopoly and raise prices? Would it have too much market power and breach competition law?

The Match Maker puts all this information together to form a view about what could happen in future. For existing offers put to the market, they can form a view about the likelihood of success and invest accordingly. Education courses may exist that focus on the relevant law and micro-strategies and can aid this process. It may seem like investors could spend all their time looking for potential and actual mergers and takeovers. At certain periods this could be true, as this activity tends to go in cycles or fashions.

Match Making is a business that is dominated by consultants and their fellow-travellers. I would say that the culture in these firms suits Big Business personalities who consort with their wealthy clients. In fact, they may understand the motives of these clients the best because they are like them. The people behind the scenes who examine the details, of which there will be many, are more likely to be Intellectuals and Small Business people, who specialise in particular facets of the law, company valuation or restructures. Team Players may also be involved. They can have valuable insight into the business environment and how the market and customers might respond.

Networker

Do you have friends who are also interested in investment? You could benefit by talking with them about your plans. It is interesting how our ideas improve or dissolve when we are forced to explain them to someone else. Friends can also offer good advice or tell us why our ideas are flawed. If you are fortunate, you may even pick up some good investment ideas to follow up. Therefore, friends address the risk that we are too independent and lack insight.

It is possible to take your network of friends to another level. Are your friends also interested in the market, want to learn more and enjoy talking about their ideas? Are they prepared to do homework on an investment? Do you trust them? Do you share the same ethical values? You may have the basis of an investment club. This club is another way to use a network to develop your skills together.

The Australian Stock Exchange (ASX) has given a good summary of how investment clubs work:[1]

Clubs generally have a simple format. A group of friends, family or workmates meets regularly - usually once a month. They each contribute a set sum of money, say $100 per month, which the club members decide how to invest their pool of money through an equal voting system. Everyone has a job for each meeting such as researching a particular company or sector. Funds are generally invested via a partnership structure. Usually each member has a turn hosting the meeting at their homes, or alternatively at the local pub or sports club.

Current investment club members give many reasons for investing as a group. A core reason

---

1 www.asx.com.au.

is that club members share responsibility for obtaining investment information and making investment decisions. Investing can be a daunting process if you are starting out by yourself. The risks and costs associated with investing are shared among members.

Club members increase their knowledge about investing and how to invest successfully. Members share knowledge and benefits from other's experiences.

Similar to being part of an exercise club, being part of an investment club provides members with motivation, support and encouragement. This increases their knowledge about investing and how to invest successfully, which increases their confidence in investing.

Investment risk is reduced through collaboration and exposure to differing viewpoints. The only limits are those that are agreed in advance, like the avoidance of certain businesses or products that the club members do not like (for example, tobacco, alcohol or furs). The ASX also recommends that the club require at least two signatures for any withdrawal of funds to reduce the risk of fraud.

A famous group of Networkers is the Beardstown Ladies' Investment Club in America. A group of women with an average age of 70 joined together to invest. New members then joined as others left or passed away. This club has been quite successful as a long-term enterprise.[2]

The investment club format seems to suit Team Players and Small Business investor personalities best.

2 Mark Gongloff (1 May 2006) "Where Are They Now: The Beard-stown Ladies", *Wall Street Journal*: www.online.wsj.com.

They are used to mining their friends and contacts for information. In contrast, Intellectuals may not be willing to share their ideas and want the freedom to act on their own. Big Business personalities may be frustrated if their risk tolerance is much higher than other members and if the decisions take too long to be made.

I know there are people who believe that making money is immoral, with the exception of anyone they know. Your friends may therefore not be suitable as an investor network. Your local library, broker, newspaper or the internet may provide the names of clubs and their contact details.

Business Expert

Do you have the sort of work experience that lets you guess how businesses will respond to changing economic conditions? You may know how people in management react because you have seen it for yourself. Perhaps you have been that manager. It may surprise other people that you have not become an investor already. Much of what you know, even as general knowledge about business is useful. In fact, you learned by doing. To take your knowledge further, try making predictions as a result of the news. You probably do this already, but I mean for specific companies or funds.

For example, if a manufacturer of critical building supplies were to raise its prices, how would this affect office construction? You may be able to predict the flow on effect to outstanding projects and therefore the market price of the listed property vehicles that own them. Or if a manufacturer raises its prices, would their customers continue to buy as much as before? You may have an understanding of the customer base from working in a similar company.

A pragmatic business sense is of value in all organisations. It is an intuitive understanding of managers, suppliers and/or customers. It reduces the risk that your ideas do not work in practice due to the complexity of the risks. If you are early in your career, you may consider working in a range of organisations to build up your commercial experience. For some, this may actually be the stepping stone to a bigger vision and leadership. But for others it can still be extremely valuable for their investments.

The Business Expert focuses on an industry or business type. Company reports, media articles, analysts reports can be useful sources of information. Here are some additional questions that might be used.

- How big is the industry and what are its' major features?
- Is the industry affected by new technology? The market may need to be monitored for competition.
- Is the industry highly regulated? For example, the financial services industry never ceases to implement laws because there are changes every year. It adds major costs that impact on profits.
- Is the industry subject to major risks (see chapter fifteen)?
- Who controls the industry? Is the customer, producer or manufacturer, distributor or retailer? For example, in the Australian food industry there has been a shift in bargaining power over recent decades from producers to large supermarket chains.

It should come as no surprise that Small Business people are natural Business Experts. Big Business people could be if they have spent their career in a particular industry or have the patience to learn. Intellectuals are possibly too far removed from the business sphere, unless they have devoted themselves to a particular role.

Team Players could well have the experience, but may not be aware of how much they know if their co-workers have the same knowledge.

Technologist

Do you have an interest in technology? There is a whole field that involves watching for new developments. The Technologist is more than a science geek though. They need some of the big picture to see how this new development can benefit the community. The Technologist needs to answer questions, for example:

- Is the new technology an improvement?
- Can it be produced cheaper?
- Are its new features important to customers?
- Will the development give a competitive advantage?
- Will the value of the technology flow through to a company that develops or licenses it?

A variation on the role of the Technologist is to assess the quality of intellectual property rights. These rights are granted as an incentive for more investment. Patents, for example, give the owner an exclusive right to use an invention for twenty years. It means that they can lower the output for the invention and raise the price without fear of competition. This anti-competitive advantage can be very valuable. Patents may therefore boost the share price of the companies that own them.

Each patent application will contain a lot of scientific information that is made public. Technologists will use it to form their own view of whether the application is likely to succeed. There are several reasons why a patent application may fail. There may be no commercial uses, the invention is not new or novel, or it may not represent a sufficient inventive step over earlier inventions. Experience is valuable because these tests involve opinion. Technologists could gain experience through their work in a particular field or by reviewing the success or failure of different patent applications. They could also review a sample of applications and the outcome without putting any money at risk. It may take years to gain this experience, however.

The Technologist will examine any information about trials that is published. Trials are the practical testing requirements for certain inventions. For example, trials are legally required for medicines due to the risk to human health of inferior products. The trials may also come in successive phases. The Technologist will identify current trials and monitor for announcements closely. In contrast, other investors may simply have no real understanding of the science, patent process or results and so make poor investment decisions.

A patent is granted for twenty years, as noted above, during which time the competition can be shut out. A Technologist will therefore want to know how much time is left on all a company's patents before they invest. If the patents are nearing the end of their life, the Technologist will also want to know about the brand that has been built up around an invention. A trusted brand may allow a company to withstand competition after the patents expire.

Unfortunately, not everyone respects a patent and copycats may try to profit from it. The patent owner may take legal action to stop them and to seek damages. The offenders may respond by challenging the patent and whether it is truly valid. A lot of money can be at stake. For example, juries in the USA may award huge sums to small players who have their patents infringed by big corporations. The flow-on effects for share prices can also be sizable. This means that a Technologist who can assess the strength of a patent may predict which side will win in court. They can invest accordingly.

Intellectuals are the natural Technologists, and may

include scientists, journalists, science teachers, engineers and science buffs generally. Of course, not all scientists and so on will be Intellectuals (meet some and find out). In addition, a Small Business person with expertise in a particular area, like a software developer, market researcher or patent lawyer, could equally have an advantage over others. Big Business types may have more of a struggle to get into the technology. They may not have the interest or patience to dig deep enough and the sort of advice that is needed may be hard to obtain. But they can size up the meaning of a press announcement and act quickly. Team Players likewise may find this a challenging area unless they and their peers work in a scientific field already.

People Person

Do you have an interest in people? Are you curious about how people think, their motives and how they interact with others? A field has developed that covers psychology, culture and customer behaviour. The Big Picture Artist will consider it, the Business Expert will understand it for their area of interest, but the People Person will make it their central focus. This might seem strange, if not risky. Are not the financial performance figures more important? The Number Crunchers certainly think so and they are right up to a point. But how a firm works together, in response to competition or a crisis, is important. It may provide a competitive advantage. The financial numbers are still relevant, but can be used by a People Person as supplementary evidence. This approach could be a pleasant surprise for all those who have been turned off investing by the weight of numbers.

A great source of information for the People Person is the media. A lot of journalists who cover business may not be details people either. They substitute an obsession with profit forecasts for an obsession with chief executive officers. This is not the same as the Big Business fetish

I mentioned in an earlier chapter, though the two may overlap. It is not about worshipping Big Business people or trying to copy their style. But it does involve asking a lot of questions about how leaders influence the share price generally and in specific instances. For example, at a general level:

- What makes an effective CEO?
- How do they create a culture of success in their organisation?
- How do they respond to crisis and change?
- How do they reward their team for taking risks?
- Which organisations should be watched for sudden management changes?
- Are companies with a weak culture likely to be targets for takeover if their rivals are stronger?
- How harmful is board disharmony to share prices?

At a more detailed level, the People Person may look at individual leaders who dominate a firm and its culture. In this way, they will identify more triggers that could affect the share price. They will need to ask questions like:

- What is the background of the leader?
- Who is their successor? Do they have one?
- Who is on their executive team?
- What is the reputation of their team?
- How do the executive team relate to each other?
- What is the leader's shareholding and level of control? A substantial shareholder may be particularly difficult to dislodge.
- If an individual board member / executive team member left, would any disharmony be resolved?

Some companies are so heavily dependent on their

founder that they would be said to be a key person risk. The People Person would need to ask, for example:

- If the leader left, would there be sufficient expertise in the firm to carry on?
- If the leader left, would the firm become a takeover target?
- If the leader left, would earnings be put in doubt?
- What would be the likely market response to departures?
- Does the company have a succession plan?
- What are contract lengths for the key people?
- Are there incentives for length of service?
- What is the average age of the key people and their likely successors?
- How would the shareholders respond to key person changes?
- What sort of changes are the most important (eg. resignation and retirement)?

In short, the People Person will use their curiosity about others to build scenarios, knowledge and intuition. It can also feed into risk analysis (for example, see the discussion of sensitivity analysis in chapter twelve).

Another variation of the People Person is someone who has an interest in customers and their behaviour. The study of the retail market for products and services is a huge field. Popular trends and fashions can be highly profitable, but short-lived. Customer loyalty can build repeated cashflows and strongly increase the value of a company. For example, there are many brands of detergent available for washing clothes, but customers tend to stick to their favourite one. This loyalty adds value to a brand and the company that owns it. Plus it can show up as a premium in the share price.

Knowledge of the customer base may be difficult

to acquire, but a sense can be gained from media reports and through buying market research reports. The internet is also a vast and sometimes unpredictable source of research, but as always be careful to find out who wrote it and who paid for it. The outcome of research has been known to be skewed by commercial interests.

The Team Player is an obvious People Person in the making, they just may not know it yet. The Small Business type is another potential People Person, though for specific companies or industries in which they have experience. Other personalities may see this skill as superficial and less reliable than the underlying business. But leaders do matter to the market. This interest is a strength that can also be used to supplement other work.

Contrarian

Are you the sort of person who knows what the group thinks yet makes up your own mind? Are you stubborn enough to go with what you think is right? Or do you just plain like going the other way to everyone else? You could have the makings of a Contrarian.

A Contrarian does the opposite of what the market thinks to take advantage of cycles, booms and panics. When you hear your neighbours start talking about investing, the Contrarian starts selling. When the neighbours complain about losing everything in a panic, the Contrarian buys. In Australia there is an old farmers' saying: buy in the dry, sell in the wet. In other words, buy when there is drought and land is cheap, but sell when times are good and there is plenty of rain, grass, profits and land is expensive. A Contrarian therefore tends to wait, emerging from their sleep by a sense that the market has gone crazy once again. Then they can act with quite surprising speed.

To develop as a Contrarian, you need to understand the long term market cycles and the state of the economy and market. In general, the upward part of the cycle is marked by increases in confidence, earnings and speculation that peaks. This is followed by a reduction in confidence, earnings, leading to panic and a trough in the market. Then the cycle starts again. The cycle can also be split and labelled as the upward 'bull' phase and the downward 'bear' phase. The Contrarian goes against these phases to address the risk that either will fail.

It might sound easy to recognise a trend, or at least mindless optimism and panic, but it is surprising how we are lead by each other. The budding Contrarian therefore also needs to build independence. In the end, the way to become a committed Contrarian, as with all investing, is to test your judgement and see if you are right.

The trouble with much information about cycles and market behaviour is that it is sourced via the media. You need a lot of practice and a sceptical eye to distil informed comment from other articles, experts from sales people and research from marketing. This takes time and commitment. Central banks produce and publish economic research, which tends to be quite technical. Another option is to pay for analyst's reports. These should be available through the internet.

Contrarians are patient, long-term investors, but they must be prepared to change quickly if the economic cycle changes. A warning sign could be as simple as news of a merger that changes the economic landscape. On a larger scale, it could be news of an unexpected collapse in a key foreign market. Or there could be a hurricane or earthquake that has terrible consequences. The flow-on effects could even change the economic cycle.

Big Business types can make good Contrarians if they have the patience to hold their position. This seems unlikely. Intellectuals make better Contrarians because they have independent minds. Small Business types can be good Contrarians too because they understand the economic cycle, unless they are so immersed that they cannot see it. A small minority of Team Players can make the best Contrarians of all as they can recognise the group mood. The challenge for them is to go against it.

Summary

Investors have many strengths that can be applied to their goals. Some common strengths are:

Careful with money
- Controls costs.
- Increases the upside risk through the expansion of funds with which to invest.
- Reduces the downside risk of losing your capital.

News Watcher
- Collects commercial intelligence.
- Increases the upside risk through superior filtering of news to find relevant information.
- Reduces the downside risk of poor decisions due to too little information.

Number Cruncher
- Copes with financial numbers.
- Increases the upside risk through identifying out-performance or potential.
- Reduces the downside risk of not understanding a target due to too much information.

Big Picture Artist
- Integrates diverse information to see the big picture.
- Increases the upside risk of seeing opportunities that others have missed.
- Reduces the downside risk that too much focus is given to individual pieces of information.

Match Maker
- Sees likely mergers and takeovers and understands the impacts and benefits.
- Increases the upside risk by researching potential matches before they happen, so is ready to act.
- Reduces the downside risk associated with sudden news and being left behind by other investors.

Networker
- Shares information with a network.
- Increases upside risk through shared intelligence.
- Reduces the downside risk of individual decisions.

Business Expert
- Uses experience and intuition. They learn by doing.
- Increases the upside risk by acting before others.
- Reduces the downside risk of investing in businesses which have complex risks.

Technologist
- Understands science and its' commercial uses.
- Understands the strength of legal protection.
- Increases the upside risk from the impact of successful technology on company earnings.
- Reduces the risk of failed patents or court cases.

People Person
- Interested in people and their motives.
- Increases the upside risk through an understanding of the impact of leadership and culture on share prices.
- Reduces the downside risk caused by people risks, including the risk of losing key individuals.

Contrarian
- Invests the opposite to the market trend.

- Increases the upside risk that arises from major trend changes.
- Reduces the downside risk of those changes and not reacting fast enough to them.

Chapter Nine
Limit Your Weaknesses

Too many people focus on their weaknesses and downplay their strengths. This may be largely because weaknesses are known, but strengths are underdeveloped. Perhaps you were brought up with too much criticism, so dwell on your weaknesses. It is possible that you dismiss praise when you get it, but remember the negative comments for years. The result is that you end up with an unbalanced idea of your potential.

As I said at the beginning of the last chapter, I think a better approach is to do more of what we enjoy. Yes, we need to limit our weaknesses and try to turn them into strengths if we can. But who enjoys thinking about their weaknesses? The solution is to apply the same self-awareness that you use for your personality, risk tolerance, goals and strengths to your weaknesses. This is important because I think weaknesses tend to come with warning signs. These signs are your trigger to quickly act or avoid. Then you can get back to focus on improving your strengths in more detail.

In this chapter I have created a list of weaknesses, just as the last chapter listed strengths. Again, I have suggested some options. This cannot be a complete list, but remember not to get too obsessed with your flaws. That can be a weakness too.

Overenthusiastic

A surge of enthusiasm in some people may be linked to over-confidence and poor judgment. You may find you spend on clothes or other consumer goods when you are in this up-mood. For the investor, a similar experience can mean rash decisions made on impulse. The consequences for your savings can be dramatic and harmful.

If impulse spending is what you do, then a warning sign is the surge of enthusiasm mentioned above. Learn to recognise it, so you can decide what to do next. It may be good to have a cooling-off period and only invest when you feel calmer. It could also be useful to examine the downside as well as the upside risks. Or create a list of minimum checks that you need to do for its profits, cashflow, reputation and debt levels. Do they meet your standards? It is a bit like getting the tick of approval from yourself before you invest.

Limiting your weaknesses is not always about self-denial or kicking yourself. Try to turn your weakness into a strength. Impulse buying can be enormously rewarding if it is channelled properly. You can act on your instincts faster than most when you are in the mood and beat the rest of the market. So one way to limit the damage is to research a list of targets in advance. Then if the market price is right you can seize the opportunity. Other approaches include using small, short term investments and hedges (see chapter seventeen).

Perhaps you are addicted to spending. The pleasure of buying may in fact mask an underlying depression or low self-esteem. If this is the case, you may need professional advice to work through these issues. If you have any available capital left, it may be best invested in a way that limits your access. For example, a fund that has withdrawal procedures may suit you better than a brokerage account that allows you to trade online in an instant. It gives you time to change your mind.

Restless

Restlessness seems to me to be related to over-enthusiasm, but lacks the same drive or pleasure. Restlessness is the product of inactivity and a desire for action. In particular, there may be a mismatch between financial goals and the investment timeframe. For example, the investor may have high wealth in mind and a timeframe that is far too short. So they get impatient, which can lead to sudden, poor choices. In particular, risk may be underestimated. Your investment risk levels may therefore rise well above your real risk tolerance level.

At least Restlessness is a state that can be recognised. A growing sense of unease, boredom or a desire to fidget can be associated with sudden thoughts of investment. It may lead you to watch the market more closely than is usually necessary. Then it is only a matter of time before you feel the need to do something and the rest, I hope, is a learning experience.

A plan and a list of preferred investments, as well as triggers for investment, could be useful. If you know you have a problem with Restlessness, create a list of targets beforehand, research them, plan your trades and the price, then follow your plan when Restlessness hits. As before, write up your plan if you think this will work.

Another approach to Restlessness is to convert this energy into looking for new areas of investment. This can be the time to identify gaps in your knowledge and fill them. You may be able to benefit from written notes on why you invested, what worked and what didn't. Or this is the opportunity to investigate an entirely new field. It can be a constructive use for a weakness and is your internal reminder to not get stuck in a rut. Keep yourself busy.

Delayer

Do you have great ideas but miss out on the benefits? How many times have you thought something might happen, then it did, but you were left behind? By the time you are sure the market has moved and the profit is no more. Uncertainty is your warning sign. It is both your protector and a source of frustration. If you are not careful it can contribute to a rebound effect: rash decisions can result as you try to catch-up. However, delay could in fact be quite sensible and a strength if it is carefully applied. Here are some suggested solutions:

- Invest less of your available capital at a time, so you can afford to make a few mistakes.

- Diversify your risk with other investments (see chapter fifteen). However, if too much time and effort is needed it is also a source of risk.

- Invest in hedges as insurance against loss (see chapters sixteen and seventeen). Note hedges have their own risks too.

- A specialist course or book on a particular investment strategy you like could help. You may even develop better signals for market entry or exit (see part three). This replaces uncertainty with knowledge and hopefully an increased likelihood of success.

- Buy more certainty through an independent and qualified adviser. Their advice should be tailored to your goals, available capital and risk tolerance.

- Turn caution into a strength by using it as a trigger for learning. Then decisions can be made quickly from a position of knowledge.

Suggestible

Most people are Suggestible to some extent or there would be no such thing as a career in marketing. But some investors take suggestibility too far. Do you believe everything you read in the newspapers? Or in a company report? Or in a free investment seminar with no obligation to invest? You are open to others guiding you to meet their goals, not your own. Your warning sign is not having enough information that you understand. It may be difficult to notice if an expert seems trustworthy.

Someone who knows they are suggestible could respond with more caution and become a much more discerning investor. Here are some solutions:

- Develop a list of factors or evidence that you must have before you invest. This could include financial data, trend analysis, economic data and so on.

- Remain open to new ideas and information. This could turn your weakness into a strength.

- Does your adviser give you enough information? Is it too detailed? Do they give out the information at rocket speed so you cannot possibly digest it? Ask them to slow down, simplify and repeat yourself if necessary. It is smart to ask stupid questions.

- Seek a variety of opinions and be sure to include your friends too.

- Sometimes media commentators will run a column to answer investment questions. So ask some and use their knowledge to identify gaps.

- Give yourself more time and keep watching the news. Sometimes a favourable article will be followed by one that takes the opposite view. It is as though the article flushed out another writer who thinks differently.

- Be more sceptical. Ask yourself: What is the motive of each journalist, company official or adviser who gives their opinion? Is it likely to be affected by whether they make money from you?

Proud

Do you have difficulty in admitting your mistakes? Most of us have this weakness to some degree. A warning sign is that we tell our friends about our successes, but forget to mention the losses. Others include making excuses or minimising the impact of a loss. In particular, Intellectuals will rationalise it: "It is part of a balanced portfolio", "I expect it will rise in the long term", or "I am a long term investor." This makes a market correction sound somehow painless. Even if a loss is your fault, it is not an end to your investing career (unless you gambled the lot with no research). But clearly if you do not acknowledge your mistakes you will not learn from them. Intellectuals in particular are experts at making excuses.

The trouble is that if you do not admit what has gone wrong then you may not do anything. True, time may be all that is needed for a recovery, but there should be a positive decision to wait. You might be better off by accepting your loss and getting some money back to invest again. Even taking what you have left and putting it in a bank may be better than doing nothing.

A solution is to actively analyse the reasons for your investing results, whether good or bad. If you do this each time it becomes harder to avoid the detail of your mistakes. Yet it may also highlight what you did right as well. You may have unknown strengths that can make the process of reviewing failures a lot less painful.

Of course, if you have continual mistakes something more drastic is needed. You could benefit from a period of market abstinence and by reviewing your investment style, goals, strengths and weaknesses. More education could be useful too.

Collector

Once you have a portfolio or collection of investments, culling it now and then can be difficult. You may keep failures or investments that no longer fit your strategy. You found them, you bought them and you love them. This is the weakness of the Collector who hoards and cannot let go. Some may even get out their investment records from time to time and look at them. Your warning sign is an attachment that does not stand up to reason.

A solution is to set criteria for selling in advance. Choose a benchmark return, such as a percentage over what you would get for deposits from the bank. Or you could make a strategic decision to keep certain types of shares. This could be your reason to cull the rest that you know should really be sold.

You could turn a weakness into a strength through the use of a long term strategy. Collectors are among the best who 'buy and hold'. But this is not the same as 'buy and never sell'. You also need to include a review process. It may be triggered by a note in your calendar or an alert in your mobile phone or computer.

Another alternative is to protect the value of your portfolio. The idea is that if any of your investments are poor, their fall in value will be compensated by a rise in the value of your protection (see later chapters on risk management). This can make it easier to sell at a loss.

If you really cannot free yourself from the dead wood in your portfolio, or you know that you are a Collector with a problem, then delegation may be best. Invest through a fund, for example, and let a manager make the painful decisions for you. There may be a loss of connection with the investments, but overall this approach may give you better returns. Perhaps you could also collect something less costly instead?

Summary

As with the strengths mentioned in the previous chapter, I have risked over-simplification by listing some weaknesses:

Overenthusiastic
- Downside risk of rash decisions.
- Warning is a surge of enthusiasm.
- Solutions include a cooling-off period and checklist for when to invest.
- Turn it into a strength by taking opportunities that you identified earlier.

Restless
- Downside risk of rash decisions.
- Warning sign is a sudden thought of investment coupled with unease or boredom.
- Solutions include a plan, investment triggers and research decided in advance.
- Turn it into a strength by investigating new areas of investment when restless.

Delayer
- Downside risk of missing opportunities.
- Warning sign is uncertainty.
- Solutions include smaller investments, research, education and seeking advice.
- Turn caution into a strength by learning more. Decisions can be made quickly from a position of knowledge.

Suggestible
- Downside risk of believing too much of what you hear.
- Warning sign is insufficient information.
- Solutions include a checklist of information that you need before you invest, seeking multiple opinions and taking more time.
- Turn it into a strength by remaining open to new ideas.

Proud
- Downside risk of not admitting mistakes, so repeat them.
- Warning sign is secrecy or excuses for loss.
- Solutions include the active analysis of mistakes, market abstinence and re-education.
- Turn pride into a strength using a review process to identify other strengths for development.

Collector
- Downside risk of missing opportunities by keeping unsuccessful investments too long.
- Warning sign is an irrational attachment.
- Solutions include benchmarks for selling, portfolio reviews, risk management and funds.
- Turn collecting into a strength through the use of a long term strategy.

I am sure I have only scratched the surface of potential weaknesses. Problem gambling and stress may be relevant too and are mentioned in appendices to this book (They are exceptions rather than common weaknesses, so were not mentioned here). It is important though that you are not distracted by your weaknesses. I suggest that you use the warnings signs of weakness to take action, but spend more time on building up your strengths and successes.

Last, if you decided to write down your thoughts about your personality, risk tolerance and goals, now is the time to add your strengths and weaknesses. You may be surprised at the picture that has emerged of your investment style. It could be more detailed than you expected.

PART THREE
Investment Strategy

How to Use Part Three

An *investment strategy* is simply the methods that you use to invest. At its core is your investment style: personality and risk tolerance, aided by goals, strengths and weaknesses. But the actual strategy is how you go about investment.

Use this part to think about which of the following are right for you:

- A short or long term outlook: How long do you keep your investments for?

- Risk *assessment*: How do you understand the upside and downside risks?

- Risk *management:* Will you control risk using traditional methods or derivatives?

Part three should make how you will approach investment clearer. Some of the subject matter may be familiar to you. But my aim is that you will look at it with the self-knowledge gained from the earlier parts of this book. You may therefore better understand the methods and pick those that best fit your investment style.

Note that I mainly refer to public companies, which are those listed on a stock exchange. This is partly for convenience, but my comments may apply more broadly, including to other investment vehicles like funds and trusts. They may also apply to companies that are not listed on an exchange, but which have listed products, such as bonds, derivatives and debt-share hybrids.

Chapter Ten
Short-term Investing

Short-term investors typically invest for less than a year. They tend to get criticised more than praised, or at least that is my impression. Perhaps their returns are smaller than those who invest for the long term, it may be more risky or even a form of gambling. I am not going to survey every piece of research as I am not an academic, but I have my doubts about taking too negative a view. The fact is there are those who make a living by investing for the short term. Some are very good at it and may even work for major financial institutions. So it is not that short term investing cannot succeed. It just does not succeed for everyone or even the majority.

The skills of the short term investor are not readily conveyed in books. I suspect a lot of the success comes down to personality as much as technique. This is another reason why writers may favour the long-term approach: there is more for them to write about. For all I know, the authors have also failed as short-term investors, so it must be wrong for everyone else. I am therefore going to outline what I think about short-term investors and ask you to consider whether their approach would suit you or not.

The Trader

The *trader* is a good label for a short term investor. Traders could hold their stake for a few months, days or even a few minutes. Day traders will seek to close off all exposures within the same trading day. They are the folk who are almost glued to their computer screen as they watch prices change in the market. Their strategy requires particular skills and information that can be quite different from those who invest for the long term (see the next chapter).

A trader must be able to exploit brief opportunities for profit by being quick and unemotional about cutting their losses. They risk failure through rash decisions, loss of attention and even stress. Short-term investors must therefore develop a method that will survive repeated use at short notice. Success will also require a working understanding of companies, markets and their peers and probably some risk management.

Traders may be *short* if they sell a stock that they do not own. They can do it if there are several days until final settlement. Meanwhile, the price may have fallen. If so, the trader buys the stock at a lower price, uses it to complete the earlier sale and makes a profit. But if the price rises, they are still required to complete the trade. The trader will then make a loss and it can be large.

If too many investors (or funds) short sell, it can distort the share price for a stock. It may force the price down and even cause the market to lose confidence in a failing stock. Short sellers who cannot deliver will also disrupt the market. Short selling may therefore be regulated like a form of market manipulation (depending on your local law).

The Upside of Price Volatility

Price volatility is the degree to which market prices fluctuate. Traders can be more comfortable with price volatility than other investors. It provides much more opportunity for profits than a stock with a stable price.

Traders may act upon patterns of buying and selling that occur prior to a change in trend. Some of these form familiar shapes when depicted in a trading chart (see chapter thirteen). But greatest gains may be realised before the new trend is confirmed. By then a trader may have already exited for a profit. Or they follow the short-term trend until it collapses and then exit fast.

For example, a stock may enter a period of volatility

where the trend is horizontal between regular highs and lows. A trader may then seek to buy low and sell high repeatedly, though watching closely for another change in trend.

The Downside of Price Volatility

Price volatility is the enemy of short term investors as well as their friend. It can bite those who trade and are not quick enough to exit their positions when the market turns against them. So when it does, a surge of trading activity may occur. This seems natural to short-term investors, but to the rest of us it seems like there are too many hyperactive traders involved. Eventually, there may be so much volatility that even experienced traders retreat. The likelihood of loss at these times is just too great and the market becomes like a casino.

Another side-effect of price volatility is the effect on companies that trade. The problem is that the staff who are hired as traders may also trade for themselves. So if there is a general market correction, do they limit their own loss first or that of their employer? What would you do? A few seconds delay could cost some companies millions or more.

One solution is to ban personal trading during office hours or try to monitor it. But in a time of mobile phones and private brokerage accounts it is almost impossible to prevent. Others accept that the best traders also like to trade for themselves. In fact, it may be a form of reference when they are hired. So the risk that these traders may act selfishly at critical moments is accepted as a cost of doing business. This risk may complicate the effects of volatility on your investments.

Stress

The stress of investment can be harmful for anyone with any strategy. But I think short term investors are particularly in danger if they invest large sums. The volume at risk and the size of their losses can eventually unnerve them. Traders have been known to take their profits and walk away permanently. Or they may evolve into a different sort of investor if they cannot take the pressure. If traders are really unfortunate, the stress of the market and the values at stake can harm their health. Anyone thinking about becoming a trader needs to consider their ability to cope with stress. It is worth knowing some signs that stress is becoming dangerous in order to do something about it (see appendix two).

Get-Rich-Quick Schemes

I have to add a few words about the shortest strategy of all, the get-rich-quick-scheme. There is an old saying, "If it sounds too good to be true, it probably is". Investment schemes that offer incredible returns over a short period may suck in innocent people who should know better. Team Players are rounded up by their friends who show them their blossoming bank accounts. Small Business types exchange their common sense for an unhealthy dose of greed. Intellectuals will make note their adviser's qualifications then look no further. Big Business types will invite them all to a free seminar with no obligation to buy. Even other Big Business personalities get hooked.

A feature of get-rich-quick schemes is the urgency. You need to sign up, pay money and get involved NOW. You will also get three lucky chances to win an apartment in Lagos. Missing out is a strong incentive to act quickly. Consumer advertising uses the same tricks, but with quality goods to back it up. It is strange, but spicy illegal activity may actually discourage some people from asking too many questions. If this is your experience then you are no longer a victim, just corrupt.

In times of crisis, it may be forgotten that investors have accountability for their own actions or failure to act. It is everyone's responsibility to fully understand an investment product and ask questions or seek advice until we do. You will not be to blame for being an innocent victim of fraud, but it is our responsibility to stay away from investments that appear to be illegal.

Big Business

Big Business personalities love the cut and thrust of trading. They win when they beat the market. This profession is also very competitive. If they work for large financial houses it can be very well paid too. Big Business types really love that last bit. In return, they are prepared to work long hours under a lot of stress and so tend to party hard afterward.

Intellectuals

Intellectuals may not make good short term traders in general. They may get an outlet through the design of complex trading models. But in most cases the snap trading decisions will be based on too little information and research to make it attractive. Their risk tolerance may not stand it either. In fact, they are probably more conscious than most about what will happen if they make a mistake, or at least they may dwell on the likelihood.

Small Business

Small Business personalities can make great professional traders who live and breathe the market and its complexity. Small Business people are probably better at it even than Big Business types. They watch the market constantly and develop the best instincts for the chance of a profit and to limit their losses. They live happily as specialist traders.

Team Players

Many successful traders could be Team Players

or at least have a leaning towards this personality. These types meet and drink together, share rumours and predictions and buy the same clothes. The flashier sorts end up wearing the same uniform, depending on the fashion, which could include gaudy cuff links and bow ties. They clearly do not use the bus.

In a fast-paced market, there may not be time for detailed research, so a decision comes down to what your friends are doing, their gossip and market sentiment. In fact, traders may be prepared to take risks using sub-standard information: rumours, expectations or just a gut feeling. These are important, but if traders resort to creating rumours to generate price volatility then they may get into trouble. It could be illegal, depending on the local law in your country.

Summary

Short-term investment could last a few months, days or minutes. Short-term investors are:

- Quick, so can swoop on deals before long term investors are aware of them.

- Opportunistic and so may exploit price volatility, though as a group they may cause it.

- Risk tolerant, so can accept the risks of numerous trades, which may involve large sums.

- Able to deal with stress (see also appendix two).

- The beneficiaries and victims of price volatility. Opportunities are quickly exposed and eroded just as fast.

Chapter Eleven
Long-term Investing

Long-term investors typically invest for more than a year. They appear to have a better reputation to those traders we met in the previous chapter. Partly this is because there are so many advisers, fund managers and writers who sell to and praise them. It is also fair to say that most investors act for the long term. This is good for the overall stability of the market.

The Patient Investor

The patient or long-term approach can suit those who currently have limited information, limited interest in investing or time. It will not suit those investors with short-term expectations for profit. They need to become traders if it suits them or adjust their goals to reality.

A key difference between long and short-term investment is the importance of investments that generate income. The long-term investor will need to consider income payments (eg. share dividends and bond coupons), capital gains or losses and tax issues. This income is often not available to a short-term investor unless they time their investment right before a payment is declared. The long-term investor may therefore use different and probably more detailed research to add value to their choices.

Timing for the patient investor is often about detection of a trend. It should not be a surprise that they seek to enter the market at the beginning or a long period of price growth, then get out at the end at a profit. I deal with methods for doing this in later chapters.

In addition, long-term investors have more time than short-term traders to research and consider alternative investments. It means that it is less crucial to get the timing of market entry and exit exactly right, though it will make a difference to their profits. It also means that patient investors can develop more complex techniques if they wish. With experience, these investors may also rely on their instincts, but it is a matter of trial and error over a long period.

The Upside of the Long Term

The patient investor benefits from the continuing inflow of funds into the market. Markets tend to rise in the long term due to increases in population and their retirement savings. Even during the depths of recession money should continue to flow into the market, if only into lower risk investments like cash deposits and certain debt instruments. Investors will switch into other riskier investments as the cycle turns and confidence returns to the broader market. The market will eventually recover in the long term and these investors will be better off overall. It requires patience and enough confidence to keep up your morale during a recession whilst looking for bargains.

The Downside of the Long Term

Inflation is the enemy of the long-term investor. *Inflation* is the continual rise in prices. It means money buys less and so is worth less over time. So to be worthwhile, investments must grow in value faster than the rate at which money falls in value. In other words, the growth rate of capital gains and income must exceed the inflation rate. (Short term investors can be hurt by inflation too, but their immediate risk is more likely to be price volatility, as mentioned in the previous chapter).

Big Business

Big Business types will see the opportunity of a long-term trend and seize it. Generally, a Big Business type will do what it takes to follow through with their plans, even if this means keeping their investments until a trend peaks or staying out of the market until better opportunities arise. But the longer the period of self-denial, the harder it will become. Big Business people may have the greatest difficulty in adapting to a set-and-forget style. It can be just too tempting to do something risky and exciting. A good solution for the Big Business person is to buy the right advice and follow it, then take up a competitive sport instead.

Intellectuals

Intellectuals can be patient if their research is superior and they have confidence in it. But knowledge of how little they may know and the risks that are out there can be a limiting factor. In the absence of market experience, the Intellectual may lack enough confidence to risk everything on a long-term position. After all, they could be wrong. But when they have done enough research to be sure, the Intellectual will wait it out and not be deterred by market fear, opposite trends or common sense.

Small Business

Investment with a trend suits the Small Business type. They have a finely tuned sense of how their customers, suppliers and competitors feel and behave. Put another way, Small Business owners are used to milking a customer trend for all it is worth and it is not much different in the markets. They also know better than most that businesses go in cycles and how to exploit them. However, the Small Business type may be limited by their experience. If they specialise they may miss the opportunities that occur in the broader market.

Team Player

Some Team Players make the worst long-term investors. This is because they can make sudden and inconsistent decisions if there is a change in group sentiment. This behaviour can undermine a long-term strategy. However, those Team Players who can sense the overall sentiment of the market may make the best long-term investors of all. They can gauge when a trend is blindly optimistic and about to collapse or is strong and going to continue. In other words, they can sense the truth behind the trend. Team Players can therefore succeed as patient investors if they develop their discernment. This may be as simple as regularly reading the financial news, joining an investment club or through more experience.

Summary

Long-term investment is the identification of trends that flow from economic cycles, then exploiting them for at least a year and as long as possible. Long-term investors are:

- Patient.

- Risk tolerant, so can accept the risk of corrections around an overall trend.

- Beneficiaries of increases in population and retirement savings. Cash inflows aid an upward long term market trend.

- Victims of inflation that erodes the value of capital gains and earnings.

Chapter Twelve
Fundamental Analysis

Fundamental Analysis is the study of the financial performance of a target, usually a public company listed on a stock exchange. Investors who use this approach will pour over company accounts and related press releases. They use financial numbers to value the company and decide whether the market has under- or over-valued it. They also need to consider the effect that performance might have on any future valuation and the share price.

In practice, Fundamental Analysts use risk analysis. They choose a group of financial numbers that reflect performance outcomes, typically of public companies that are listed on a stock exchange (see examples below). These numbers are chosen for what they indicate about the upside and downside risks to the business. They also are used to compare companies and help investors pick those with the greatest upside and lowest downside risks.

The same process can be taken a step further with *financial ratios*. These ratios are calculated from a comparison of different financial numbers. It results in fewer numbers and so simplifies the comparison of companies and industries (see appendix four for examples). As a result, the investor who uses Fundamental Analysis and financial ratios can look at more companies and scale-up their research.

In addition, I will look briefly at two common sub-sets of Fundamental Analysis: value and growth analysis. These are used to identify the best prospects for upside risk. Investors may use one or a mixture.

Fundamental Performance

Fundamental Analysts use a range of financial numbers or performance measures. These numbers reflect certain financial risks to investment performance. The ones chosen are up to each individual investor and may be the product of trial and error. They can be found in annual reports, profit announcements, analysts reports and newspapers. Some of the commonly used numbers include:

- Earnings, profits and cashflow.
- Debt levels, interest rate charges and tax.
- Working capital for operations and expansion.
- Financial ratios (see appendix four)

In all cases, Fundamental Analysis is used to identify future upside risks and looking out for potential downside risks. For example, changes to earnings may reflect risks that have become reality, including changes to market demand, size and growth, government policy, etc. Debt levels and interest rate charges may reflect risks to the business if it cannot extend finance to expand or even to survive. Note that investors may have factored these risks into the investment price already.

The focus of the Fundamental Analyst will depend on the nature of the businesses that they target. For example, it is pointless using cash flow measures for a mining exploration company that will not make any money for years. In contrast, for cash and bonds, the analysis will necessarily be more limited if the income is fixed. In that case, analysts may compare the value of returns of different bonds relative to their market prices.

Valuation

A Fundamental Analyst may take current and projected earnings and costs (including interest charges on debt) then calculate a value for the investment over a reasonable period, such as 5-10 years.[1] A smaller period may be needed if the projections are too rubbery

1 The calculations, for example of Net Present Value, can be complex and could form the basis of a whole book.

to be reliable. By creating this valuation, the investor can compare it to the current price. They may decide to buy if an investment is undervalued and sell if it is overvalued. Or the valuation is used to identify a trading trigger if it were reached.

Part of the valuation process is that the Fundamental Analyst has to consider their level of confidence in the available financial data and projections. Obviously it is in the interest of companies to talk up their prospects. Likewise, analysts and advisers with a conflict of interest will do the same. But if the Fundamental Analyst lack confidence in the numbers that are published, it may prompt them to avoid the stock or investigate it further.

Sensitivity Analysis

Sensitivity analysis is a useful tool to speed up risk analysis and decision-making when circumstances change. The Fundamental Analyst imagines different financial numbers to those that have been reported or are expected. Perhaps they will imagine a range of risk scenarios related to financial performance. This involves thinking both about what could go right in future (eg. market expansion, less competition or a patent application is granted) or wrong (eg. fewer sales, high interest rates or a patent is successfully challenged). The investor then has to think about the likely effect these scenarios would have on the financial numbers and their valuation. This assessment may draw on past history within the company, similar companies, the investor's own experience and so forth.

The results feed into the same valuation method used by the investor before. This should produce a series of valuations for different scenarios. If those scenarios happen, the investor will be able to act quickly. They can buy or sell the stock depending on whether the market price is above or below their valuation.

If different scenarios actually happen, the sensitivity analysis may still be useful as a point of reference. The investor will know what the broad effects of an event will be on their valuation and trade accordingly. It means that the investor can make faster and, on the whole, better decisions.

For some investors, speculation about mergers and acquisitions is the ultimate form of sensitivity analysis. A merged entity may yield differing *synergies* or benefits not possible if the entities remained separate. These synergies can flow through to costs, profits, financial ratios and the share price. For example, the combined entity could yield cost savings from combined management teams, properties, production facilities and marketing spend. Historical examples may provide some guidance.

On the other hand, the investor must consider that there are synergies or conflicts which are non-financial. For example, the corporate cultures may mesh or be too difficult to make a merger successful. The changes may also be driven by careful leadership and common sense or ambition and fashion.

In addition, two sub-sets of Fundamental Analysis have emerged: the value and growth approaches. They reflect the emphasis that is put on financial numbers and future scenarios, so are relevant to sensitivity analysis. Investors use these approaches to seek bargains (value) or prospects for financial expansion (growth). Much has been written about value and growth, with partisans to match. My aim is not to support one approach over the other, but to ask, "Which suits you?"

Value Approach

The value approach uses financial numbers to identify bargains. It is assumed that the market will discover the value of a stock and the price to give a superior return. Unfortunately, the reason why a company may be good value is because it is poorly run, with an incoherent strategy, a drunken CEO, inferior quality control and unhappy customers. A basket of law suits may also be on the way. These problems could mean that the market never holds a better view of the stock. More than good value is needed, but these numbers can be a trigger for more research into the downside as well as the upside risks.

Growth Approach

The growth approach uses financial numbers to identify the best prospects for earnings, profits growth or return on capital etc. The idea is that growth in the numbers will flow through to the share price and capital gains. Trends and financial ratios may be used to simplify the analysis.

Generally, the Fundamental Analyst is concerned with quality of earnings, meaning they are repeatable, plus the potential for growth. For companies, the following may also be attractive: dominance in a market niche, superior management, superior culture, intellectual property rights and a growing market.

The growth Fundamental Analyst will want a low price as much as anyone else. But they may be prepared to pay a relatively high price to get exposure to the best growth stocks and future gains. In short, they are more interested in a fair price for an investment, given its potential, rather than the cheapest bargain.

Unfortunately, the future is uncertain, markets disappear, management disagree, competitors or substitute products emerge. Growth investments therefore need to be closely monitored to ensure that they deliver. A growth spurt in share price that cannot be explained may also mean that a reversal is about to happen. Investors might be wise to review that business more closely for the downside as well as the upside risks.

Big Business People

Big Business people learn what they need to about Fundamental Analysis so that they understand what their advisers are talking about. They may start in this area if they have a bent for numbers, but move to a much larger field of view with success. I am thinking particularly of accountants who end up abandoning their calculator and become company directors. They can interrogate their financial officers in detail at board meetings. Big Business types may also be attracted to financial ratios (see appendix four), which simplify the decision-making process and aid decisive action.

Intellectuals

Intellectuals probably would not find numbers satisfying on their own, unless they become involved in delving into what lies behind. More research about irregularities might satisfy their analytical minds. Forensic accounting is therefore a field that could interest them. The limit is the amount of information that is made public.

Small Business People

When I think of Fundamental Analysis I have to admit I think of Small Business personalities with a strength in numbers. True, anyone with an aptitude for details and numbers can perform this research. But the Small Business type can live and breathe the sensitivity analysis in a particular business or industry. They are the specialists whose experience can simplify the risk assessment process.

Team Players

Team Players who like numbers may be hired to count up them for their employers and analysts. The question is whether they can use this skill for themselves. It may help them to discuss the results with their peers, friends or advisers. Each will contribute opinions until the consensus view of the fundamentals for a company is formed and how it compares to the alternatives.

Summary

Fundamental Analysts like:

- Reading financial numbers and accounts.

- Details.

- Investigating reasons for the numbers.

- Using financial numbers to value a company.

- Sensitivity analysis, which is about looking at how different risk scenarios affect the numbers.

- Merger and acquisitions, which is about looking the combined earnings, profitability and potential savings of different company combinations, etc.

Fundamental Analysis is used to assess risk through:

- Value or the potential for a market correction.

- Earnings growth potential.

- Discrepancies in the numbers.

- Confidence in the numbers.

Chapter Thirteen
Technical Analysis

Technical Analysis a form of risk assessment that is based on market behaviour. Technical Analysts look for price trends, or repeated price movements in the same direction. They also look out for patterns of investor behaviour that may indicate the risk that a trend is about to change. As a result, future prices may be predicted and an investment decision can be made.

Technical Analysis does seem to get its fair share of bad press. The evidence is criticised and it has to be said that trends alone may look flimsy. Of course, it might be that critics are all Fundamental Analysts. They prefer their own discipline, oddly enough. A better idea, in my opinion, is to use Technical Analysis if works for you.

Technical Data

Technical Analysts know that market movements can be caused by a huge number of factors, including good old irrational behaviour. So they look at market movements, not the reasons behind it. This is good news for people who hate reading financial accounts.

Here is some simple data that anyone can collect (or possibly buy):

- Opening prices
- Closing prices
- The range between the daily high and low price
- Price trends
- Trading volumes
- Volume trends
- Angle of the price or volume trends
- Rate of change in price or volume (momentum)
- Time period over which a change is noticed

A lot of data is collected, so the Technical Analyst will compile a chart to make sense of it all. The result is that complex trading history is simplified to a series of dots over time. Perhaps these dots can be joined together to form a line that shows a *trend*, or directional price movement. This trend can then be extended in an imaginary line to predict future prices. Investments can be made accordingly. The danger is that risks, and the trends which reflect them, can change.

Trend Lines

A price trend will vary, forming highs (peaks) and lows (troughs) around the overall trend line that rises or falls. These variations are how the market tests the trend. A series of higher peaks and higher troughs can confirm that an upward trend is place. In the same way, a series of lower troughs and lower peaks can confirm that a downward trend exists. The exact point at which a trend is confirmed is up to you, but a series of three peak and trough repetitions seems to be sufficient.

Over time, the trend lines may form familiar patterns or shapes that warn a Technical Analyst of changes to come (see some examples later in this chapter). The trouble is these patterns are not fool-proof. They may indicate a cross-roads, when the market is uncertain. The final outcome could be that the trend changes or resumes. The analyst must therefore be wary at such times and look for other indicators for confirmation (eg. trading volume). There is a danger that Technical Analysts will believe in their patterns a little too much and become over-confident, ignoring the potential for other outcomes.

Momentum Indicators

A problem with historical data is that there can be so much volatility that no meaningful trend is seen. Volatility can, however, be reduced through averaging the data for a period. For example, closing prices may be averaged for a twenty day period. Next, the price from the first day is deleted from the set, the price from the twenty first day is added, and the average is recalculated. This process is repeated over subsequent days to form a series of averages, or *moving average*. These averages can then be plotted on a chart to create a trend line, known as a *moving average indicator.*

A moving average indicator is useful for showing momentum. It is a measure of market confidence that may spillover into future prices. So a rising moving average line may be used to predict increased confidence and further price increases. A falling line may indicate that a price reversal could happen, if it has not happened already.

Moving averages are a useful predictive tool, but are not fool-proof. The market may reverse so the momentum indicator backtracks. The period used for averaging can also mean that the indicator is too sensitive or not sensitive enough. Technical Analysts address this problem by using more than one indicator. For example, they may use a short period (eg 20 days) and longer periods (60 or 90 days) to calculate the moving average. The result will be several indicator lines. Some investors use a cross of these lines as confirmation of a trend change and as a trigger for trading. Even so, caution about market reversals is still needed.

Other Volatility Indicators

Another use for volatile market data is as an indirect measure of risk. At a company level, volatility in share price may be compared to that of the market generally to give a number called a *beta*. The trouble is that the investors as a whole will never use betas to drive market movement. Market behaviour is more complex than that. So care must be taken to depend on them to make decisions.

On a broader scale, volatility in markets may be used as a general indicator of market sentiment. The Volatility Index (VIX) produced by the Chicago Board of Trade is a well known example (see appendix three). The VIX could support other Technical Analysis that indicates a trend has paused and could be about to change.

Short Term Outlook

Technical Analysts who have a short-term focus may exploit the same changes as patient investors, but sell out earlier and move on. They will also seek to exploit a temporary correction within an overall trend. For example, they may spot that two bonds with similar terms and yield trends are out of alignment and seek to profit from the difference. In doing so, they could help to bring the bonds back into alignment. In addition, short-term investors may seek to exploit the start of new trends using patterns or shapes in the chart (see later examples).

Long Term Outlook

Technical Analysts with a long-term outlook will be particularly interested in trend developments. Is it strengthening or weakening? This information lets the investor know how long to hold their position and adds to their confidence.

A trend may accelerate if the peaks or troughs increase in size. For example, the peaks of a rising price trend may grow bigger and bigger compared to the size of the troughs. Trading volumes may also increase on the price peaks and decrease during the troughs. This could show that the rising price trend may continue. Long-term investors may monitor these sort of effects as part of deciding whether to keep or sell out of an investment.

Distortions

Some stocks exhibit their own price patterns. This may be because a large number of investors share the same behaviour. Over time, this behaviour can become self-fulfilling as investors recognise that history repeats. They buy and sell according to their memory of what went before and so reinforce a particular pattern.

In addition, the price history and trends of some major stocks may be distorted by institutional investors, such as funds. The effects of large, lumpy trades on the market can be significant. It may seem that there has been a change in market perception of risk and a new trend, but in fact it is just a temporary distortion. A wise Technical Analyst needs to closely monitor trading volumes and for sudden trend reversals.

Investment Personalities

Any of the investment personalities can become an effective Technical Analyst. Basically, anyone who does not like accounting or who does not get a thrill from numbers may gravitate to this field. It can provide information at a glance for the Big and Small Business types or give the Team Player a wider source of information - the market - if they are branching away from relying on their friends or advisers. Intellectuals may get involved out of curiosity, but I suspect there will not be enough detail to satisfy them. They will find it unfulfilling or too risky to trade off a pattern of sales that looks like a flag or a mountain. Some Small Business types too may prefer to thoroughly understand the financials of their favoured stock before they invest. Technical Analysts do need to be comfortable investing their money just on the basis of behaviour. On the whole, I suspect Big Business types who are not Number Crunchers will be the most comfortable with Technical Analysis.

Technical Triggers in More Detail

Technical Analysts use a variety of patterns to guide their investment decisions. Whole books are written on this subject, so the examples given below can only be an indication.

A number of the patterns use a *resistance* line, drawn through the peaks, and a *support* line, drawn through the troughs (see examples below). Price movements that break through either line may indicate a trend change. Sometimes the breakthrough is so great that the old resistance line becomes the new support line (and vice versa). Care is needed though because the change could quickly reverse.

Here are some examples that are highly stylised. In practice, there would be a lot more price volatility.

Triangles or Pennants (see diagram below): a wide variance of peaks and troughs narrows, so that the resistance and support lines come together. The result looks like a triangle or a pennant (a triangular flag). Eventually the price should break through one of the lines to signal the direction of the new trend.

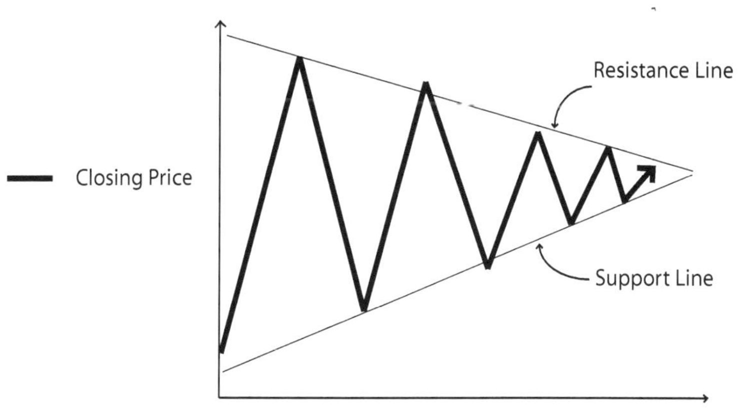

Rectangles or Flags (see diagram below): peaks and troughs may be about the same size, so the resistance and support lines run roughly parallel. It could mean that the market is unsure. The side-ways pattern is resolved when the price breaks through one line.

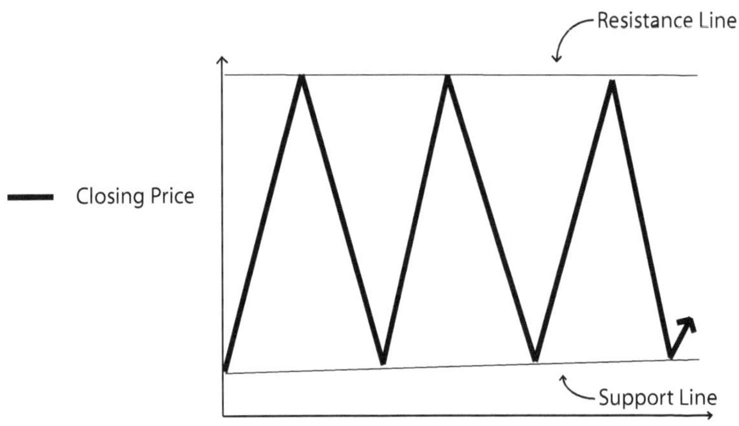

Head and Shoulders (see diagram below): two peaks in an upward trend are challenged by a third peak which is lower. A new support line then emerges. When it is broken by a further price fall it indicates a change in trend (an example of a *breakthrough signal*).

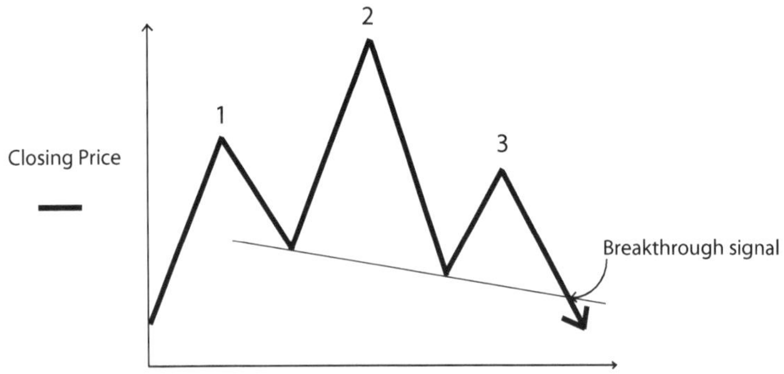

Reverse Head and Shoulders: is the opposite of a Head and Shoulders pattern. A new resistance line is formed. Then an upward price breakthrough signals the start of a new upward trend. Investors may be keen on this pattern in a recession.

Double Top (see diagram below): is like the Head and Shoulders pattern, except there are only two peaks of about the same height. A new support line is formed and a breakthrough signals the start of a downward trend.

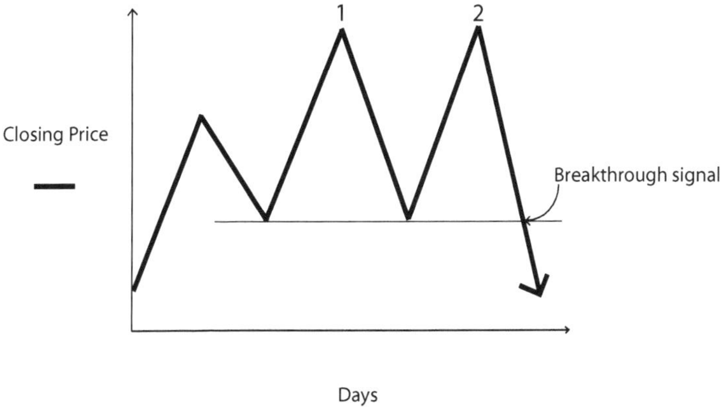

Double Bottom: the opposite of a Double Top and signals the start of a new upward trend.

A word of caution: just because price breaks through a particular line it is not a signal to bet your life savings on a new trend. Markets may change their mind and what seems like a new trend may evaporate. It may be better to wait for several more peaks and troughs to confirm a new trend. Trading volumes may also be considered and whether they increase in coming days. It is a sign that the trend is accelerating and will continue By then the immediate profits may have been missed, but is probably less of an issue for a long-term investor.

Summary

Technical Analysts like:

- Data collection, as they are prepared to collect a lot of price data, find it on a brokerage website or buy it.

- Visual images, as market behaviour may be expressed as a recognisable pattern on a chart.

- Big picture trends or repeated movements in behaviour that can be used to predict price changes.

- Limited information, so that market behaviour is used to guide decisions (other information may be used too).

Technical Analysis is used to assess risk through:

- Trend lines, which show directional price movements. These trends indicate how the market views current and future risk.

- Shapes and patterns on a chart. Recognising them can reduce the time and effort needed to make an investment decision.

- Support information (eg trading volume, momentum).

Chapter Fourteen
Hedge Spread Analysis

In this chapter I look at a form of risk assessment that can be called Hedge Spread Analysis. It is a variation of the Technical Analysis that was discussed in the last chapter. Hedge Spread Analysis uses a risk *management* technique called hedging, but for risk *assessment.* It is chiefly used to consider risks, not to control them.

Hedge Spread Analysis uses a price signal created by the difference in price of an asset and its' hedge, defined below. This signal can help investors find investments with the best returns relative to the market perception of their risks. However, it is a *guide* only.

Definitions

Before I describe how to use a hedge spread, I need to define a few terms.

- A *hedge* is an investment with risks that balance those of an investment (eg. shares). If you lose money on the investment, you will gain money on the hedge or vice versa. In this way, your upside and downside risks are balanced to some extent. The hedge cost is also much smaller than the investment cost.

- A *specific hedge* has risks that are opposite to the chosen investment (or close to opposite).

- A *market hedge* has risks that are linked to broader market activity, such as an index (see appendix three).

- A *derivative* is a financial product with risks that derive value from an underlying asset (eg. a share) or a market indicator (eg. an index). Derivatives can also be used as specific or market hedges, depending on how they are structured (see also chapter seventeen).

- The investment-hedge spread *(or hedge spread for short)* is the difference between the price of an investment (eg. shares) and its hedge (eg. derivatives). It highlights how the market sees the risk of the investment. It is limited by basis risk.

- *Basis risk* is the risk that movements in the investment price do not match with movements in the hedge price. Some hedge price changes may have nothing to do with the investment. For example, some derivatives may have a limited life. Their value may drop dramatically as they are about to expire. Or there may not be enough buyers and sellers (see liquidity risk, below). Or speculators and large funds could distort the hedge price.

- *Liquidity risk* is the risk of how quickly an asset can be turned into cash. Investments and hedges may be liquid with enough buyers and sellers. Otherwise, prices may be distorted. The usefulness of the hedge spread will therefore be reduced if there are not enough buyers and sellers for either the investment or the hedge.

Important note: it is assumed here that the markets for the investment and the hedge are liquid. Basis risk **must** *be considered by the investor in each case.*

- A *Stable Hedge Spread Trend* will appear on a chart as a horizontal line. It means that the investment and hedge price movements offset each other.

- A *Widening Hedge Spread Trend* will rise on a chart. It means that the overall share price and hedge price trends are moving apart.

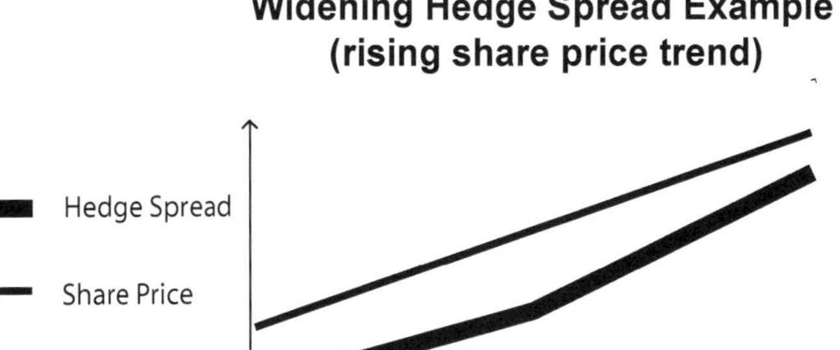

Widening Hedge Spread Example
(rising share price trend)

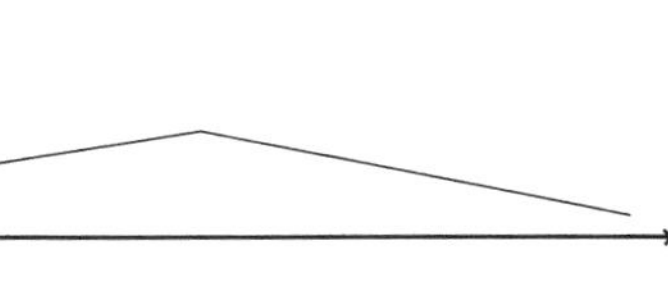

Days

- A *Narrowing Hedge Spread Trend* will fall on a chart. It means that the overall share price and hedge price trends are moving closer together.

Narrowing Hedge Spread Example
(falling share price trend)

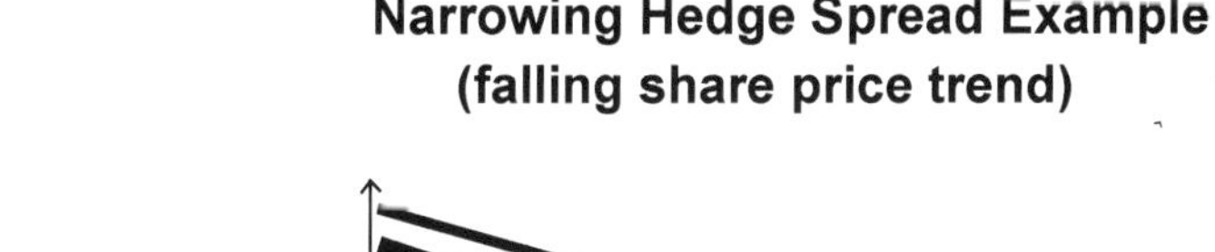

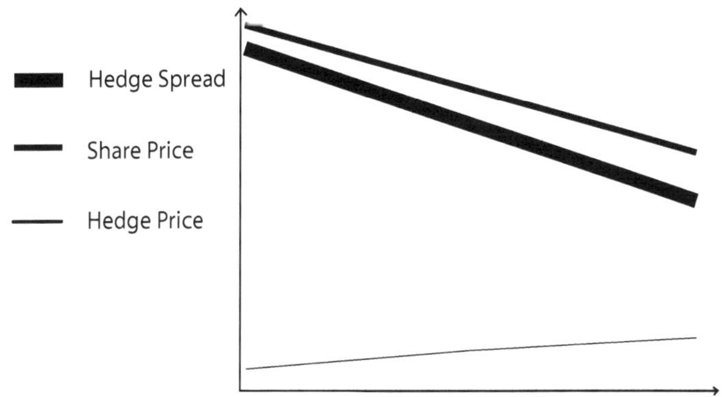

Days

Note the previous two graphs are very stylised. In practice, the prices and spread would vary a lot more, which is why the trend lines may be useful.

Interpretations

In the following examples, I have suggested some interpretations for when an investor is *long* in a stock (already holds it).

	Hedge Spread	Interpretation
Rising Share Price Trend + Falling Hedge Price Trend	Widening	Investors buy fewer hedges. Indicates more confidence in upward share price trend. Potential buy / hold decision.
Rising Share Price Trend + Rising Hedge Price Trend	Narrowing	Investors buy more hedges. Indicates less confidence in upward share price trend. Potential sell/ avoid decision.
Falling Share Price Trend + Rising Hedge Price Trend	Narrowing	Investors buy more hedges. Indicates more confidence in falling share price trend. Potential sell/ avoid decision.
Falling Share Price Trend + Falling Hedge Price Trend	Widening	Investors buy fewer hedges. Indicates less confidence in falling share price trend. Potential buy /hold decision.
Rising or Falling Share Price / Hedge Price Trends	Stable	A possible crossroads in market sentiment. The hedge spread should be monitored for change.

As above: remember to consider basis risk. Hedge spreads should not be used in isolation.

Multiple Comparisons

In theory, investors could create a number of hedge spread charts with the same investment and different specific hedges. This comparison could show how investors generally view the risks associated with that investment. Or market hedges could be used to assess the broader impact of market risk.

In addition, investors could repeat the process for other investments. It could help them identify those which offer the best returns given their risks (as seen by the market). Fundamental Analysts, for example, might use a list of targets which appear to offer the best bargains or growth prospects. Others might use financial ratios to select a short list of targets for Hedge Spread Analysis and comparison.

In practice, time and the amount of data would limit the number of charts that can be made. The market for both investments and hedges can move quickly as well, so the charts become outdated quickly. Nor are these charts fool-proof and so should not be used in isolation, as I have warned throughout this chapter. Therefore, Hedge Spread Analysis may have more potential than real value at present.

On the other hand, the cost of Hedge Spread Analysis could be reduced by brokers and others, if they have not done so already. Many websites already provide automated charts, momentum indicators and financial ratios, some for free. These services could extend to hedge spread charts too. If so, more complicated comparisons might be possible, such as hedge spreads for an industry, momentum indicators (see chapter thirteen) or hedge spreads where both the investment and hedge are derivatives.

Investment Personalities

The sort of personalities who are attracted to Technical Analysis could be attracted to this variation of it as well. My hunch is that the added complications of Hedge Spread Analysis may attract more Intellectuals. Others will follow if software or brokers assist with the charting process. They may not have a detailed knowledge of derivatives or pricing models, but could still benefit from the signals created by these spreads. They may also use it as a supplement to different methods of risk analysis.

Summary

Hedge Spread Analysts could like:

- Hedging or the balancing of risks between an investment and another financial product.

- Data collection, where price data must be collected and charted over time in order to identify trends.

- Visual images, where trends are identified from charts.

- Big picture trends and predicting where asset prices are heading from price signals and trends.

- Limited information, so that market behaviour is used to guide decisions (along with other information).

Hedge Spread Analysis may be used to assess risk through:

- Pricing signals that are a guide for risk assessment.

- Trend lines, which are repeated price movements in

the same direction, including hedge spread trends.

- Support from other risk assessments. Hedge Spread Analysis is subject to basis risk, so that the spread is affected by issues other than the risks of the underlying investment. This emphasises the need for confirmation.

Perhaps you read all the warnings about basis risk and liquidity risk in this chapter and came to the conclusion that Hedge Spread Analysis is too vague. There could be many other interpretations of a spread and reasons why it changes. It may also take too much time to conduct Hedge Spread Analysis for it to be useful currently. On the other hand, I suspect that there is potential for Hedge Spread Analysis to be used more in future, particularly if the calculations are provided through the websites of brokers and others.

Chapter Fifteen
Risk Category Analysis

Risk Category Analysis is another means of risk *assessment*. It can guide better investment decisions, as an addition to Fundamental Analysis, Technical Analysis and Hedge Spread Analysis. However, the scope of enquiry here is far broader. *Risk Category Analysis* is the study of every conceivable upside and downside risk for an investment (eg. a company). To simplify the process slightly, these risks are put together into common categories.

It is true that a Fundamental Analyst may look behind the financial numbers to assess their strength or unusual results. Fundamental Analysis may therefore result in targeted risk investigations. Technical Analysis and Hedge Spread Analysis can also be used to identify unusual market behaviour for further risk investigation. But Risk Category Analysis is more systematic in how each risk category is considered in turn. In this way, the Risk Category Analyst may consider more risks than the other risk analysts.

Risk Categories

Risk categories are needed due to the complexity of risk. The investor may be tempted to think that they have thought through all the relevant upside and downside risks and overlook something important. The advantage of categories is as a tool to make sure the investor considers the key risks for an investment.

There is no universal set of risk categories. One of the best lists made so far was created for the revised Basel Capital Accord. Under this Accord, banks around the world must assess their risks in order to work out how much capital they need to hold for emergencies. This capital (it includes reserves and forms of debt) means that banks can meet their legal obligations, like withdrawals. Otherwise, everyone may worry that they will lose their savings if the bank were to collapse. This fear could lead to a 'run on the bank', where depositors all try to get their money out at the same time. It could actually cause the bank to collapse. So banks hold capital for emergencies, and the more risk they have, the more capital they must hold. It means that they need to make risk assessments and so need risk categories to make sense of it all.

The Basel Accord focused first on the credit risk that bank loans would not be repaid. Later it was realised that banks get a lot of income from fees and market investments that have nothing to do with loans. Eventually, a revised Accord was issued in 2004. It covers three overall risk types:

- *Credit risk or* the risk that each borrower will not repay their loan.

- *Market risk* or the risk that market-based invest-ments may be hurt or helped by market price movements.

- *Operational risk, which* covers risks relating to the execution of business requirements. Complicated definitions are possible, but basically it is an extremely broad range of risks.

Some residual risks are not covered by the Accord and include the risk relating to business strategy.

A list of operational risk categories was prepared for the revised Accord. (There is different methodology for looking at credit and market risks, but it may not be relevant for many investments). The list should be available on the Bank of International Settlement's website.[1] There

---

1 See Bank of International Settlements (2006) Annex 9, Detailed Loss Event Type Classification, in "International Convergence of

are seven main categories:

- Internal fraud
- External fraud
- Employment practices and workplace safety
- Clients, products and business practices
- Damage to physical assets
- Business disruption and system failures
- Execution, delivery and process management

These categories are then split into further sub-categories for the financial services industry, but they could apply more broadly. There is also no reason why other industries cannot develop their own list, an industry standard, if they do not have one already. You could create your own checklist of risks too, though the list given above is a good starting point. I am confident that risk categories, and the analysis that goes with them, will continue to develop.

Using the Categories

A Risk Category Analyst will go through each of the risk categories one by one and consider what can go right or wrong. For example, what is the rough likelihood of an event (eg. external fraud) in a particular business and what could be the potential impact? To answer this question, the analyst may be able to use some published examples of losses. They will have to watch the financial news closely or pay to access a news database. The result will probably still be a high level estimate. In fact, they may get no further than a 'high', 'medium' or 'low' likelihood and impact. This estimate should not be a problem for a private investor. They use Risk Category Analysis to form an overall view for an investment and whether it should be bought or sold.

Capital Measurement and Capital Standards: A Revised Framework - Comprehensive Version": www.bis.org.

For example, you might see a news item about how a financial institution sold complex investment products to retail customers (This would fall under the category of "clients, products and business practices" and a sub-category called "suitability, disclosure and fiduciary"). You might then focus on the impact of court cases, regulator fines, remediation costs and the importance of a good reputation. Once other relevant risks are considered, does it affect your view on whether the stock of that institution should be bought or sold? What if the damages claims were substantial and there was insufficient insurance? Would that alter your response?

Risk Category Analysis is different from the analysis we looked at in earlier chapters. It may not give precise triggers for action. Rather, a lot of different information is brought together. Investors use it to form an overall view of the upside and downside risks for an investment. Obviously this view will be influenced by your investment personality and risk tolerance as well.

In addition, it should be obvious that to research risks and different scenarios could use a lot of time. As a result, do not bother with a tidal wave that hits far inland. Stick to what you believe is realistic. Certain risks may then stand out. Clearly banks are subject to fraud risks. Mining companies have a focus on operational risks relating to exploration, refining and transport. Office blocks that are above a fault line are more exposed to earthquake damage. Brokerage firms may have a focus on sexual harassment and so on. These risks should be your first focus as you gain experience.

Restricted Information

A major flaw with Risk Category Analysis is that the sources of risk information are restricted. Companies will let you know all about their upside potential of course, but not their stuff-ups, mistakes and incompetence. In fact, investors will often not know about the downside risks unless a disaster occurs that is so big that it cannot be hidden or must be disclosed by law. These disasters include major IT failure, labour strikes, terrorism, building collapses, fire and major fraud. The rest of the time a Risk Category Analyst needs to have a relatively high risk tolerance to make decisions with such limited information. Most investors probably have it already out of ignorance.

A source of risk information for investors in public companies is the annual report. It may specify the largest costs that are associated with risks that became reality. For the most part, however, these costs will be buried in expenses and the discussion will be bland. I expect that the company would say it takes risk very seriously, whatever that means.

A few organisations will go a bit further and report on risk benchmarks. For example, mining companies may report on the rate of staff injuries. This disclosure lets investors and staff know about the company's commitment to improve. It may even pressure staff to be more careful. Another example is to publicise the test results for a business continuity plan, which sets out how a company will continue in business during a crisis and afterward. This too may give investors comfort.

Advisers who have experience or expertise in a particular company or industry are a valuable source of risk information. They will know what the risks are even if the companies do not make them public. The problem for investors is to pick a knowledgeable adviser, so ask questions about their experience.

Last, there are exceptions where some risk category information has been made public. One is patent information that is relevant to someone with strength as a Technologist (see chapter eight). The risks associated with this information may fit under the risk category of "Clients products and business practices". Then there are media reports about boards, major shareholders and other key people. They are relevant to someone with a strength as a People Person (see chapter eight). The risks associated with this information may fit under the risk category of "Employment practices and workplace safety".

Risk Profile

If you decide to write up your Risk Category Analysis, each company profile should be no more than a page or two.[2] List the relevant risk categories, then add the upside and downside risks that you have identified. You may wish to describe the sources of those risks, if known. If you are able to make high level estimates of impacts and likelihood then add these in as well.

Do not waste time at the start by fussing over which risk to put in which category in the profile. You will build your own habits to achieve a consistent process in time. The same evolutionary approach could also apply to the high level estimation of likelihood and impact. It is more intuitive than a precise science at this point. *Note that this situation may change if common interpretations of risk categories emerge.*

Please note that a written risk profile has no value other than what you give to it. Some may find the process of writing it down allows them put their thoughts together. Others may find It useful as a reminder months or years later of why they wanted to invest. This can work best if you have a number of investments to remember. It can also be useful to hold yourself to account for your failures or to reinforce the basis for your successes.

Big Business

Big Business personalities will focus enough on risk to identify any major obstacles in their way. They will therefore scan the list of risk categories and consider

---

2 The profile produced by a company would be more detailed, in part because it has more information than you do.

any that jump out at them. However, I do not expect that Big Business people will live and breathe this subject. It takes too much time and they might have to socialise with some tedious types to get enough information.

Intellectuals

Risk Category Analysis should be the home of the Intellectual. Unfortunately the limited nature of public information could put them off. An exception are those Intellectuals who work as risk advisers or who have other expertise.

Small Business

Certain Small Business types may, in my opinion, make the best Risk Category Analysts. They may supplement the limited information available with work experience. As indicated earlier, this experience gives an intuitive guide to what can go right and wrong. Small Business types are also more likely to want to know everything about businesses in their chosen field. This all includes their upside and downside risks. The discipline needed to produce a risk profile may help them to integrate this knowledge and experience and make the most of it.

Team Players

Team Players can make great Risk Category Analysts. Team Players are good at getting the gossip on how different companies manage risk. Staff move between companies, word gets around and the Team Players come to know. It could even lead to a risk profile that is based on a group view, as in an investment club (see chapter eight).

Summary

Risk Category Analysts like:

- The big picture and will consider many risks.

- Diverse information, so consider a range of evidence for risk.

- Thorough analysis, so consider risk in a systematic way (risk categories).

- Balancing the upside and downside risks.

- Making decisions with limited information. Risk Category Analysis is used to assess risk through:

- Systematic consideration of risk categories.

- Formation of an overall view of the investment For companies, it includes how well risk is managed.

I appreciate that the potential for Risk Category Analysis is currently limited. There will be many reasons for public companies and others to restrict the release of information related to risk. However, I do not see these restrictions as concrete barriers. In the last part of this book (see chapter nineteen), I will come back to how this form of analysis may grow in importance in the future.

Chapter Sixteen
Traditional Risk Management

If most people think about risk management it is probably to try and stop the worst from happening. However, risk management can be about enhancing the upside as well as minimising the downside. In this chapter, I set out some of the more common alternatives for managing both the upside and downside risks.

Surplus Cash Management

One of the simplest risk management approaches for investors can be overlooked. Investors need a plan for their money when they have sold investments and no other opportunities seem to exist. This might happen at the peak of a price boom, when everything is expensive, or in the depths of a trough when it is not clear how much further that prices will fall. The danger is that investors will exit an investment then re-invest even if there are no better alternatives. Short-term investors will especially benefit from actively managing their surplus cash between trades. Restless investors could also benefit. It is therefore a good idea to have a plan for how to invest any surplus capital.

Some investors keep a cash account in which to deposit their funds between trades. Banks typically offer these accounts with low interest rates, so a better solution is needed. Brokers may offer interest yielding accounts, or some internet-based bank accounts may have high yields and allow money to be transferred cheaply.

Available Capital

Your *available capital* is how much you have to invest. It may highlight what you are prepared to lose and may be associated with a *capital buffer*, or money put aside in case of emergency. I discussed available capital and a capital buffer in chapter seven, so will not repeat myself here. But I note that the use of them is a basic form of risk management

Entry and Exit Price Triggers

The triggers for market entry and exit are prices that guide investors to buy or sell. These prices are decided in advance and are used to make quick and profitable decisions (see chapters twelve and thirteen in particular). In addition, it may be possible to develop a second set of triggers, which are used to *manage the risk that the earlier risk assessment was wrong or needs to be updated.*

For example, an upper trigger may be identified, above which the price movement would be suspicious. Perhaps news of a major profit upgrade or merger changes the value of the investment. Likewise, a lower trigger may be identified, which if the price fell below it could indicate a disaster or trend reversal. The choice of trigger should therefore be just outside the range of historical or expected price volatility.

The need for a review will often be obvious even without a trigger. An example is an earthquake that wipes out a factory. The effects on profits and the share price will be immediate. However, there may be circumstances where economic performance and the share price deteriorate more slowly. The investor may not identify an event that triggers a review, so a price trigger is useful. Otherwise, the investor may just let the matter drift until it is too late and opportunities to enter or exit are missed.

Long-Term Investment

Long-term investment for more than a year is actually a form of risk management. It is based on the assumption that markets rise in the longer term, despite short-term corrections. This is assisted by the continued inflow of retirement savings, which was mentioned in chapter eleven. A long-term outlook therefore addresses the upside risk of exploiting a long-term trend and the downside risk of selling out too early or at a loss.

Natural hedge

A *specific hedge* risks which are the opposite, or near opposite, of your target investment. It may be purchased deliberately to offset the risks of that investment. In contrast, a *natural hedge* is one that is created through the investment itself, without you having to buy something else. It will exist even if you did not intend to manage any risks.

For example, a company may make income in local and foreign markets. A weak local economy could mean few local sales (downside risk). It could also cause a fall in the value of the local currency. As a result, any foreign income could buy more of the local currency and so would be worth more (upside risk). A natural hedge could therefore exist through the exchange rate.

Note that the risks in the above example are not perfectly hedged. There are many more forces that could have an impact on the exchange rate and company income. Natural hedges may therefore exist for a period, erode and return.

Competitor hedge

Sometimes competition may create a hedge for investors even though the competitors don't mean to do so. A *competitor hedge* is based on the idea that a market has a limited size. This means that if one competitor gains market share, then one or more of the others loses. So the risk of investing in one can be hedged by investing in all the competitors.

A competitor hedge is rarely perfect. It will erode with a decline in the overall market, changes in customer demand and new competition. Investors must therefore monitor the competitors and business horizon carefully.

Gold

There is nothing magical about gold that makes it useful for risk management. It is simply a rare metal that is known for its beauty and because does not rust. The demand for gold has generally outstripped its supply, so it continues to have value. This feature makes gold an investment on its own, but it has another feature that makes it useful as a hedge: its' historical role as an international currency.

Gold was used as money for centuries, as most people know. A problem though is that gold is bulky and heavy, which tended to hamper trade. So in modern times, paper currencies were developed and backed by gold deposits. In fact, central banks used to issue credit in proportion to the amount of gold that they hoarded, even into the last century. Now central banks have sold their gold stocks, but the memory of a time when gold meant stability still lingers.

Market memory is important in a crisis and investors will often turn to gold as though it were a refuge. This is a self-fulfilling myth. Investors buy into gold because they know others have in the past and believe they will again. This action pushes up the gold price, which buffers a fall in the rest of the market. The effect is compounded by short-term traders who bet that history will repeat. The outcome is another contribution to the market memory of gold as a *market hedge*.

Fear retreats eventually and the need for gold as a market hedge will erode. Investors may find that their gold hedge is no longer useful and that they even have lost money. Caution is therefore needed about using gold as a hedge. Likewise, gold investors need to be alert for the effects of gold hedging. A surge of hedging could distort the price of gold and gold stocks. If gold investors set a risk management trigger (mentioned earlier), this surge could lead them to review their position.

Diversification

Diversification is commonly used to manage risk. The investor chooses investments with risks that are so different that it is highly unlikely that they will eventuate together. In the long-term, therefore, diversification can be useful to reduce an investor's downside risk, although the upside risks are reduced too.

A diversified portfolio of investments is composed of investments with differing risks. Generally cash is thought to be less risky than other investments, particularly if bank deposits are government guaranteed. Of the remaining types, the rough order of increasing risk is probably debt, property, shares and derivatives, but much will depend on the actual investment and how it is structured.

Part of the benefit of diversification arises from using investments with different economic cycles. For example, property and shares may have peaks and troughs of activity which can, at least temporarily, be out of sync. A loss in one may not lead to a loss in the other. In fact, it may lead to a gain as investors flock to a better performing investment.

If the economic cycles of different investments become aligned it could create a concentration of risk. The portfolio may then need to be rebalanced through a shift of emphasis to different investment types. For this reason, it pays the diversified investor to review their portfolio periodically. There is no set rule of how often to do it, but it should be decided in advance so matters are not left to drift.

Managed Investments

If you are unsure about how to diversify your risk across different investment categories, then there are professional managers who will do it for a fee. Or they will concentrate your risk according to their strategy. The choice of a manager is a way to manage the downside risk that you don't know enough about investments or don't care.

Managed investment is a broad term that covers different legal vehicles, such as mutual funds and investment companies. Investors use a pooled investment structure to share ownership, income, capital gains and losses, as well as any transaction costs. The rules of these vehicles vary, including whether they are listed on an exchange.

Managed investments are typically arranged as a collection of investment categories like cash, debt, property, shares and so on. The weighting of your investment in each option should then depend on their underlying risks and your risk tolerance. A good adviser will also adjust this allocation for your changing needs, means and age. Or you could do so following major life changes, such as marriage (if you have that option) and children.

Among the funds, there are active and passive approaches. In an *active fund*, the managers research and seek out the best investments according to their mandate. The *mandate* is a document that sets out the manager's powers and duties, as well as the method they will use. Partisans for active funds claim that the skilled manager can beat the market, particularly in the long term. Critics say that active managers cannot find enough opportunities when they have huge sums to invest. On the other hand, a smaller active fund could be more flexible and swoop on bargains. A lot will depend on the talent of the manager, but their identify and level of experience may not be known by the investor.

A *passive fund* is potentially simpler and cheaper than an active one. Investments are typically selected according to their weighting in an index. An example is to use an index of companies with the greatest *market capitalisation,* or share price multiplied by the number of shares. Money is reallocated as companies move into or out of that group. Supporters might argue that passive funds are cheaper than active funds. This is because fewer trades may be needed, so investors pay less commission. They also claim that passive funds have better performance in the long term.

The trouble with passive funds is that there may be no assessment of how well the entities in which they invest manage risk. There may also be a lag time until the stock is reassessed or an index is recalculated. Meanwhile the price may have plunged in a crisis. At least an active manager could have sold out if they were quick enough.

Debt Financing

Debt financing is the use of borrowed money to fund investment. Typically shares are bought on credit that is secured by a portfolio of other assets. Whether this is really used to manage risk is debateable, but it is an approach that is widely used. It will at least increase an investor's upside and downside risks.

If the value of the portfolio falls, the lender may require more security or collateral. This can take the form of a 'margin call' for cash. Or the lender may simply sell off the portfolio to reduce their credit risk exposure. The borrower may still be left with debt. As a result, debt financing is generally not suitable for most beginners.

Legal structures

The legal structure that you use for investing will likely affect your tax liability. Tax is a downside risk for investors, but the upside for accountants and tax lawyers, bless them. Your choice of legal structure is therefore a risk management decision that affects the returns of your investments. It may be worth seeking some independent and qualified advice if you are in danger of making the tax authorities too happy.

Some investors use a private company to make their investments (Note that for once I am not talking about a public company listed on a stock exchange, but your own company). This choice has its origins in a legal structure developed to encourage business people to take risks. It is in the national interest that these business people have the opportunity to start again if they try a business and fail, unless they are so corrupt that they are barred from doing so. An incentive of a company structure is therefore limited personal liability for the owners. The personal assets of directors may be protected if the company becomes insolvent, subject to their conduct and the local law.

Another common investment structure in a number of countries is a private trust. This is a legal vehicle that evolved out of a desire to protect a party who was at a special disadvantage. An example is the use of a trust to manage the inheritance of a minor. Trusts may have an extensive and complicated set of rules that require the named parties, the trustees, to administer the trust on behalf to those parties that benefit from it, the beneficiaries. In doing so, various risks may be reduced for those beneficiaries. I will not go into these rules that may vary from country to country. But they may include tax benefits that make trusts an efficient way to pass assets, including investments, from one generation to another.

Important note: please seek independent and qualified legal advice if you have any concerns or questions about the right legal structure, if any, to use for investing.

How Much Risk Do You Manage?

Risk management, depending on the method, can

severely eat into your investment returns. The cost is the price of various products (eg. hedges), transaction costs, plus the lost opportunity to buy other investments and make more income. The skill of risk management is to balance the greatest opportunity and the least cost. There may be mathematical models that will find this point, but I think it is more a matter of personality, risk tolerance and, eventually, of experience.

The pricing of your target investment and its hedge can be as simple or complicated as you want to make it. Here are some considerations and questions:

- Do the likelihood and impact of the risks associated with the investment and the hedge mirror each other? If they balance perfectly then you would make no profit. The losses of one would simply cancel the gains from the other. Some risk must therefore go unhedged.

- The downside impact of your investment is the cost of any losses. This is the maximum amount you need to hedge, but it will be smaller than that in practice. This is because there is not a 100% likelihood of realising a loss. Otherwise, why would you invest? Clearly, the smaller the likelihood of loss, the less you need to hedge.

- If you are uncertain about the risks, you may need to increase your hedge spend to cover the risk that you have made a mistake.

- Generally risk rises over time because of uncertainty about the future. It may pay you to therefore have a series of hedges with different time periods.

- Is the hedge available and affordable? Others may

have hedged already and this pushes up the price. There may be other drivers as well, unrelated to hedging. You could sacrifice too much upside risk if the hedge cost is high. You may have no choice except to leave the risk unhedged or choose another investment.

Investment Personalities

Big Business types seem to me to be among the first and last in a community to manage risk. They are first because they will embrace new methods before their competition. They will learn what they need to learn about hedging and diversification, then move on. They may also use gold as a hedge and sell quickly once the trend changes. On the other hand, many Big Business types will be among the last to manage their risks because of their high risk tolerance. Many would rather leave their risks unhedged and spend more money to make more.

Intellectuals can understand the value of a hedge, but unless they understand the details, they may prefer a basic diversification approach that they know well. An exception is if they learn about hedging and the various products used for this purpose in detail.

Small Business personalities will have a capital buffer as their basic risk management tool. They may be attracted to a competitor hedge, particularly if they specialise in a particular industry with few competitors. Like the Intellectual, they will want to know thoroughly how the hedge works, but can back up research with experience that gives them an extra advantage, like an intuitive sense of when to exit the market.

Team Players are not likely to hedge unless it is recommended by their adviser or friends. The chance of that seems remote. They and some of the others may be exposed to diversification through their mutual fund and just not remember it.

Summary
Traditional risk management includes:

- Surplus cash management that is used to invest money when better investment opportunities are not clear.

- Defining your available capital and any capital buffer. You decide how much you are prepared to lose.

- Investing for the long term addresses the risk of shorter term corrections.

- Defining entry and exit triggers for the review of earlier risk assessments.

- Natural hedges, which exist within an investment without the need to buy extra protection.

- Competitor hedges, which involve investment in a range of competitors, so if one loses, the other(s) benefit.

- Gold, which is an investment that regains value during a crisis for historical reasons.

- Diversification, which is the use of investments with different and opposing risks. If one investment loses, the others may gain, and so risk is reduced overall.

- Debt financing, which is the use of borrowed money to increase both the upside and downside risks.

- Legal structures, which may reduce downside risk through legal means, such as companies or trusts.

- Basic risk management questions, which investors may ask themselves.

Chapter Seventeen
Derivatives

Derivatives have been around for centuries, but I doubt if they were ever talked about that much. Derivatives also have a bad reputation, no matter how many times you explain their usefulness. Complexity doesn't help and it is easier to be afraid of something that you do not understand. Nonetheless, derivatives have their uses as investments and for risk management. It is worth finding out something about them.

Derivatives, as the name suggests, derive from something else: an asset like shares, commodities and bonds, or a market indicator like an index. If an asset is involved, a derivative will typically give the investor some rights over it (eg. the right to buy or sell). The exact nature of the rights will depend on the type of derivative and its' terms and conditions. For example, the *strike price* is a price threshold, which if passed means that the derivative can be used. Some examples are set out in appendix six.

Synthetic derivatives can be created over assets that are imaginary. For example, synthetic bonds can be produced that do not exist in the real world. The bonds can be structured to create exposures to specific risks, or combinations of risks, such as interest rates, payment frequency and currency. The investor therefore invests in those risks. Synthetic derivatives may also be linked to market indicators, such as an index, or economic indicators like exchange rates or interest rates. These derivatives derive value from market or economic risks.

The price of a derivative will generally reflect the value of its' terms and conditions, the underlying asset and its' risks. It is also subject to *basis risk*, which is the risk that movements in the derivative price do not correlate with that of the underlying asset. Investors who buy derivatives therefore buy exposure to a range of risks, either as an investment on its own or as a hedge (below). In this chapter, I am mainly concerned with the use of derivatives to *manage* risk and so with *hedging*.

Specific Hedges

As noted in earlier chapters, a *specific hedge* has risks that mirror your chosen investment. The risks are opposite, or close to opposite, to that investment. For example, an investor who holds a stock risks that its' price will fall. This risk can be offset by the use of a put option that conveys the right to sell that stock if the price falls beneath a certain level (see further appendix six).

Market Hedges

A *market hedge* is used to guard against a change of trend for the whole market. This hedge is useful because no matter how much research you do or how confident you are, a credit crisis, flu pandemic, terrorism or some other disaster may occur that massively damages your portfolio. Provided the market still exists, a market hedge could provide some protection against extreme events. It may also be useful insurance in case of a recession that depresses the whole market.

Gold is a traditional market hedge, but derivatives can be used too. For example, a long-term market hedge can be created by using a synthetic derivative that is tied to the value of a market index. If there is an adverse market movement it should show up in the value of this index. If the index passes a threshold (agreed in advance) then the derivative can be sold for a profit. This profit should offset the market loss on other investments, depending on how much was hedged.

In addition, a synthetic derivative may be linked to economic factors like inflation, interest rates or foreign exchange levels. Strictly speaking, these are not market hedges, but would still probably influence the broader market. Investors may prefer this sort of derivative if any of these economic factors have been identified as a major risk for their investments.

A short-term investor could use a market hedge in association with a series of trades. This is because they make too many trades to hedge each one. It would take too long and be too costly (assuming the hedges were available). So the trader uses one market hedge as their short-term positions are still exposed generally to the risk of a market fall.

Long-term investors will have fewer positions than a trader, so have more time to research the right hedge. Even so, a specific hedge may be too costly or not exist for their chosen investments. There may also not be enough buyers or sellers to make a market for this hedge. In contrast, a market hedge may be more common and so less costly to obtain. There may also be more buyers and sellers, so it can be traded more readily.

Hedge Your Home Loan

Many people use a home loan with a floating interest rate, which goes up or down with the market rate. The most common way to hedge against interest rate rises is to use a fixed-rate loan. Generally these are more expensive than a floating rate.

In theory, it ought to be possible to hedge a home loan using interest rate derivatives. The exercise price would be the interest rate at which your mortgage repayments become truly painful. That is when the derivative needs to make money. A series of derivatives may also be needed to cover repeated interest rate rises. However, these one-off profits may not fully offset the long term cost of interest rate rises.

Interest rate derivatives naturally have a cost that may mean they are available only to wealthy investors.

These costs could in theory be shared between investors in a fund that bought these sorts of derivatives. Even so, a borrower would only use this approach if it is cheaper than a fixed rate home loan, which seems unlikely given the widespread use of these loans.

Risk Exposure Issues

As mentioned in earlier chapters, an investor would not want to perfectly hedge their assets, even if this were possible, or there would be no profit left. All the gains would be balanced by losses. Some other issues that are more specific to derivatives include:

- Investors naturally believe in their investment, even though they hedge it. This faith could make it hard to choose a derivative with a realistic strike price.

- The number of buyers and sellers for derivatives, *market liquidity*, should be considered. The investor may not be able to buy the hedge or sell it even if the strike price is met (*liquidity risk*).

- The deadline for the expiry of a derivative is important. The closer it gets, the more illiquid the derivative may become due to fewer buyers. It may be better to sell the derivative much earlier (assuming the strike price has been met), when there are still buyers for it, even if the full benefit is not realised.

- The investor may correctly predict the future price of an asset, but it may not be reflected in the price of the corresponding derivative, or basis risk, mentioned above.

- A market hedge may be chosen if no specific

hedge is available, or other investors have pushed its' price up too far.

- A series of derivatives with different strike prices and durations may be chosen to allow for different risk scenarios.

- The higher the price of derivatives, the less money is available for actual investment. This is a major constraint. The investor may choose instead to go unhedged or invest somewhere else.

- Your personality and risk tolerance are the ultimate guide for how much risk you hedge.

Mixed Purposes

Derivatives can be used as investments as well as for risk management. So investors may be tempted to include derivatives for both purposes in their portfolio. The trouble is that they may then forget and use a derivative for the wrong purpose.

For example, derivatives that were bought as long-term investments (eg. warrants) could be used as a hedge when there are short-term losses. The benefit of that investment may then be lost. Or long-term derivatives were bought as a hedge, but they were treated as an investment instead. Perhaps the hedge failed, but the derivatives were kept. In both cases, the investor might have been better to cut their losses and move on. Beginners may therefore prefer to use derivatives as an investment or a risk management tool, but not both.

Summary

Derivatives may be used to manage the risks of investments through hedging. Specific hedges have the opposite or near opposite risks to an investment. Market hedges reflect broader market risks that may affect the investment as well. There are a number of considerations for the choice of derivatives as hedges, which include:

- The strike price at which the derivative can be used.

- The number of buyers and sellers for the derivative, whether it is available and if it can be sold even once the strike price is met.

- The derivative life span. A series of derivatives may be useful in situations of uncertainty.

- Opportunity cost, as the investor could potentially be better off to invest elsewhere.

- Personality and risk tolerance.

More unusual variations of hedging include interest rate derivatives, which could potentially be used to hedge another major investment, the private home, if cheap enough. However, care must be taken not to confuse use of derivatives as an investment and as a risk management tool. It could lead to convenient decisions, self-deception and poor outcomes.

Chapter Eighteen
Your Strategy

The last eight chapters have provided a brief overview of different methods for investment:

- Timeframes: long or short term investment.

- Risk assessment: Fundamental, Technical, Hedge Spread and Risk Category Analysis.

- Risk management: traditional and derivatives.

Some lucky people will know or have quickly found what suits them best. For example, they will know that they have a long-term outlook, prefer Fundamental Analysis and diversification to manage their risk. Others may be intrigued by new ideas and need to think about it. I hope this book will, at the least, encourage investors to choose topics about which to learn more.

For most of us, it is worth revisiting our investment style, including our investment personality, risk tolerance, goals, strengths and weaknesses. If you wrote this information down it could be time to review it. What timeframes, risk assessment and management methods seem to fit what you know about yourself? For example, you could be:

- A Big Business person with a high risk tolerance, good-sized available capital, skills in cost management and as a Number Cruncher. You might want to look more closely at short term investing, Fundamental Analysis and a market hedge that uses a synthetic derivative.

- An Intellectual with a high risk tolerance who has sufficient available capital and Contrarian tendencies may choose to learn about Hedge Spread Analysis. Your research may be so thorough that you choose little if any risk management.

- A Small Business type with a high risk tolerance in industries in which you are a Business Expert. You also decide you have enough available capital and a capital buffer in order to invest. You may take a long-term approach, use Fundamental Analysis to compare key competitors and build an appropriate hedge using a combination of shares and derivatives.

- A Team Player with a low risk tolerance, some available capital, strengths as a People Person and News Watcher. You may do some long term investing that it based on an assessment of certain companies with key people risks and their corporate culture. You may use Technical Analysis to time your entry and exit from a stock, but otherwise invest through a fund that manages risk by diversification.

There are many more variations. This diversity of investment styles is a good reason to use the methods set out in this part as guides, not laws, and to seek additional viewpoints. Do not be afraid to review your chosen strategy. Change it if it does not make the most of your strengths or is not enjoyable. Remember, our goals and risk tolerance will also change as our family commitments evolve and we grow older.

PART FOUR
Future Risk Analysis and Management

How To Use Part Four

This part is just an extra. It will not make you invest better today. Instead, it is about a range of improvements to company risk management. Companies which are not good at risk management may be tempted by high-risk, high-profit ventures that prove to be unstable. This instability can lead to a financial crisis.

The improvements include:

- Better risk disclosure by public companies.

- Central banks charge commercial banks a different interest rate according to their risk profile.

- Bonuses should be linked to risk management as well as returns.

- Leaders should be encouraged to build corporate culture and ethics even further.

Note that I refer to public companies for simplicity. My comments could apply more broadly as well. Note also that the suggestions made in this part build on existing arrangements. The novelty lies in the combination and extent of the proposed reforms. A reason for this approach is that it is not possible to replace the entire leadership of every public company and start again. We need to improve what we have in order to avoid another global financial crisis.

Chapter Nineteen
Risk Disclosure

Disclosure is whatever the company directors tell their investors. The annual report to shareholders is a familiar example. Another is the offer document that gets issued for a financial product.[1] The contents will depend on the law and market rules. Generally, some information about the risks to the investor is included.

Risk is a combination of the likelihood of an event and its' impact (see chapter five). For example, how likely is X and how much damage would be caused if it were to happen? Some events may be so unlikely that they cannot reasonably be considered. An example is a tidal wave of sea water far inland. But a realistic risk should be disclosed to investors if it is significant enough or a *key risk*.

I want to use this chapter to suggest how key risk disclosure could be improved. Better disclosure could help investors to make more accurate risk assessments. This includes Risk Category Analysis (chapter fifteen) and Hedge Spread Analysis (chapter fourteen). Investors could then add to the pressure on companies to improve their risk management. Investors should improve their own risk management too.

Company management will dislike some of the ideas outlined here. But if faced with inevitable change, those managers will talk like they were in favour all along. Well, when they talk to regulators anyway.[2]

As before, I will refer to public companies for simplicity, but the suggestions could apply more broadly.

---

1 For example, a hybrid of debt and shares that is listed on a stock exchange.

2 A *regulator* is a body which monitors compliance with certain laws or regulations and prosecutes wrong-doing. For example, government agencies and stock exchanges may have regulatory functions.

Key Risk Disclosure

In my opinion, the disclosure of *key risks* to all shareholders should be like that used for certain investment products. The threshold could be:

What investors would reasonably need to know about an investment's risks in order to make an informed investment decision.

What is a reasonable need and what is an informed decision? It is enough for investors to decide whether to invest, keep or sell out of an investment. Interpretation of what is "reasonable" for investors to know will depend on local law and practice in each country. It need not include unrealistic risks. But it may not be the same as what the company management think investors need to know. The assessment has to be taken from the *point of view of the investor.*

Investors should know about the key risks of a particular firm before they invest, as for any investment product. They should also be informed if those risks change. This need doesn't go away once they have written out a cheque or made a bank transfer. Therefore, the same standard of risk disclosure should apply to ongoing disclosure by public companies.

Companies may prefer to rely on their annual report to communicate with shareholders. Typically these reports have bland statements along the lines that the directors take risk very seriously. I suspect that not much is disclosed and that bad news is sanitised. Some though may go further and outline a few of the risks faced by the company, depending on local law and market rules.

Public companies may argue that they already make enough ongoing disclosures under the relevant market rules. Generally, markets require a press release in which information that would affect the share price is disclosed. Examples include major earnings revisions, major risks to earnings, changes to senior personnel, major restructures, settlements with a regulator and major disasters. The trouble with the market rules is that it may be too easy to avoid disclosure. The logic is that nothing is price-sensitive until it happens, so nothing is said. Legal advice may also be sought, which allows more delays until the problem goes away. It is therefore possible to avoid disclosure and no rule is broken.

In fact, public companies may already share many of their upside risks with the public. So investors get risk disclosures now, but biased towards good news. It would be preferable to include the downside risks too, so investors are not misled. If investors can assess the upside risks then they should be able to cope with the downside risks as well. The more common these disclosures also become, the less likely it is that the market will be spooked. Or less likely that short-term traders will find opportunities that arise from fear and panic.

It is possible that a false market could be created if risk disclosures were premature. However, risk analysis skills would be encouraged if these disclosures were made on a large scale. Experienced investors, fund managers, journalists and professional analysts would more likely see the risks for what they are, without creating a false market. Companies would still be free to remind everyone that risks are just that, not facts. They can also update their risk disclosure for new information on a timely basis. This would reduce the chance of a false market even further.

Even if investors would benefit from better risk disclosures, companies may still prefer to manage their reputations with secrecy. Some form of regulation will then be needed, so public risk disclosures are made. One legitimate exception would be the need keep contract negotiations secret until they are finished. Another is that disclosures should not be required if it forced the company to break a law.

Key Risk Profile

It would be useful if *companies published all their key risks in a risk profile for their investors*. The profile would use risk categories like those introduced in chapter fifteen. One advantage of using categories is to ensure a thorough, step-by-step risk assessment, where risks in each category are considered. If companies came to use the same categories, then it would allow investors to quickly compare the risks of their investments.

Some of the risks to a company will be obvious and will never leave the profile. Banks, for example, are subject to fraud risks and this will not disappear. Even so, investors still need to know how companies do battle with these expected risks. There are opportunities here to show investors that the directors have these risks well managed (discussed below).

Some companies may pretend that they have no risk because it is transferred to their sub-contractors, suppliers or joint-venture partners. This is true insofar as legal liability is agreed in a contract. But if the supplier fails to deliver, the broader impacts and their likelihood must be considered in the profile (eg. reputation damage and loss of market share). *Risk cannot be fully outsourced.*

The process for risk assessment is up to each company. It may use industry research, loss data (see below), workshops with staff, professional opinion and so forth. Depending on investor demand, I see more scope for the following disclosure of *key risks*:

- Risks within named risk categories.
- Potential risk impacts in dollar terms (discussed below).
- High level estimates of risk likelihoods - obviously

most key risks have a low likelihood or more companies would be harmed or collapse.

- Risk expenditure, for example to fix disasters or prevent them.
- Risks related to borrowing conditions, for example debt rollover deadlines and interest rates.
- Risks related to suppliers, joint-venture partners and related businesses.
- Identification of priority risks for improvement.
- Success stories of risk reduction.
- Risks updated for business growth.
- Emerging risks.

Some companies may be surprised (and relieved) to find out how few key risks they really have. Others may be more defensive because their investors would not have realised just how risky the business really is.

The last issue of emerging risks may cause the most tension. It may be argued that this disclosure is already required. For example, the directors of Australian public companies must issue an annual report, which refers to the prospects for future years.[3] To the extent that some rules covers emerging risks then a specific disclosure requirement should not cause extra work. And, as noted above, the market could become used to timely risk updates on a large scale.

The process could be made easier through the use of a *key risk profile standard* akin to the accounting standards. This industry standard (or standards) could cover issues of classification and interpretation, the period over which risks should be considered, as well as how and when to disclose emerging risks. This is necessary so that the risks of different investments can be compared quickly and reliably. Investors can then select companies that suit their risk tolerance.

3 Section 299A(1) Corporations Act 2001 (*Commonwealth of Australia*).

I expect that a sign-off process for the profile could operate in parallel to that for the financial accounts, which is well-established in many countries. For example, in Australia, the chief executive officer and chief financial officer of each public company must sign off that the financial accounts for the period (a) comply with the accounting standards, and (b) represent a true and fair view. Directors and auditors make declarations too.[4]

In the same way, the chief executive officer, chief risk officer, the directors and auditors could sign off on an annual key risk profile. This profile should be provided to shareholders as part of the annual report or online. It may then be updated for emerging risks as required by the industry standard.

If this proposal were adopted, a public company could be prosecuted if their key risk profile did not meet the legal sign-off requirements. For example, if they did not comply with the relevant industry standard, or the profile did not amount to a true and fair view (or whatever standard is used in your country). Regulators could monitor these profiles for compliance with the industry standards.

Critics of risk profiles and disclosure will question the value of doing it and the cost. True, a risk profile will *not* help a company manage its' risks better. This is because those risks should be known and managed already. In that case, a risk profile should be very easy to set up. The advantage of a risk profile then is to help obtain loans or more money from investors. But if risks are not well-known, surely any sensible company would want to do the risk assessment? Another reason for the same work is if the directors are not comfortable that they understand these risks or that they are being managed

---

4 Sections 295A, 295(4) and 308 of the Corporations Act 2001 (*Commonwealth of Australia*). An *auditor* is someone who is paid to examine financial accounts. Some audit firms may offer risk advisory services as well.

effectively.

A risk profile clearly involves set-up and education costs. It can take time to do the initial assessments that are used to create it. But once the profile is done, the cost of updating it may not be so great, unless a bureaucracy is created that needs to feed itself. If the administration costs can be kept down, most staff will wonder what the fuss was all about.

Even so, too many risk assessments could lead to paralysis-by-bureaucracy. It may interfere with the risk-taking and profits that investors actually want. It is also possible that the assessment costs could create a barrier to market entry. A small company may decide not to list on a stock exchange if these costs are too great. A balance therefore needs to be found between the costs and benefits of risk analysis. A generation of investors is also needed who understand that trade-offs are involved. There is no point demanding the most thorough risk assessments if you are not prepared for the impact on costs and profits.

Controls

Once a public risk profile is released, a question will arise about how far the company controls should be disclosed. First, some more explanation is needed.

Put simply, a *control* is what is put in place to stop a downside risk from becoming a reality. A company may have a whole network of controls that are related. Examples include:

- The review of financial accounts for error or fraud.
- The separation of billing and payment functions to prevent staff fraud.
- Internal checklists to cover any steps needed to comply with the law.
- Policies and training to prevent mistakes.

- Reporting to management is a control that keeps junior management alert (or even awake at night). Mistakes are more likely to be corrected if the boss is watching.
- Contracts set out who is accountable for what.
- Controls are reviewed or tested by auditors.
- Risk disclosure rules are monitored by regulators and breaches can be penalised.

If something goes wrong, the company will look at the controls. Did they work or was there a failure? Was there a gap? What is needed to stop this error happening again? The biggest errors with the largest impacts should be reported to senior management or even the board of directors. They are entitled to expect that a plan of action or options will be put to them.

Internal reports must be honest documents if they are to assist directors and senior management to make decisions. Internal reports will therefore contain more control information than is ever made public. In addition, there are some controls that much remain private because they are trade secrets (eg. fraud controls). As a result, the *disclosure of controls in a key risk profile should not be legally required*.

On the other hand, investors need to know how well the impacts of key risks are controlled. It may drive companies to disclose enough about their controls to give investors confidence. It may also drive companies to seek more innovative controls and sell their skills to investors. Risk management could become part of a company's brand (if it is not already). Investors may then be prepared to pay a higher share price. Shareholder meetings may yield better information about risks and controls too.

Loss Reporting

So far I have suggested that key risks should be

disclosed to shareholders, but that the disclosure of risk management controls should be voluntary. Now I want to turn to another form of disclosure: loss reporting.

Loss is the damage caused to a company that is caused by downside risks that have become reality. Financial losses include lost revenues, compensation to customers, lawsuit costs, increased insurance costs and as well as the money needed to fix a problem and prevent it from happening again. There are also losses that are not readily measured in dollar terms. For example, it can be costly if management attention is taken away from other parts of their business. Loss of reputation and brand damage can be difficult to count as well, though they may show up as a fall in the share price.

There are good reasons to focus on dollar losses even though non-financial losses exist. Actual costs can be less open to interpretation than something vague like reputation. Dollar losses are therefore a good marker of errors, frauds, mechanical breakdowns, fire damage, union strikes and so on. They may also be detected later on by the auditors. Therefore, directors can get an idea of the company reporting culture if their auditors find lots of unreported losses.

Losses may be due to control failures or gaps as well as events like natural disasters. They need to be recorded and watched as it is one way a company keep an eye on its' costs. On a bigger scale, databases are already used to predict and manage similar losses elsewhere. Companies, investors, funds, regulators and journalists may subscribe to a database to learn about risks generally. It could be a useful source of information for Risk Category Analysis and other forms of risk analysis (see part three).

The contribution of loss data may be voluntary. It means that some companies may free-ride off the disclosures of others and report little or nothing. So an obvious question is, "Should all losses be made public?" I don't think so because shareholders do not need to know about minor errors. An exception is if these errors are large or common enough to be disclosed under rules set by the board.

My preference is that the *company sets a threshold for public loss reporting that is also published.* Investors should know what to expect and can sell their shares if they think the company is too secretive and might be hiding something. The directors would then need to watch out for investor sentiment and their competitors. Investor feedback could give an incentive to manage these losses better. An industry standard or market rules could also be useful, if not used already, for reporting losses or near misses.

Summary

Risk disclosure is about the release of a company risk profile and updates to investors. If public companies were required by law to make more risk disclosures, investors may gain more practice and become better at risk analysis, including Risk Category Analysis (mentioned in chapter fifteen). It should flow through to their actions and provide valuable feedback to companies.

Companies with poor risk management should be punished by investors for their failures. Other companies, which demonstrate consistent risk management, should be rewarded with a higher share price. This feedback is unlikely to be a complete solution, but it is one way we may avoid another global financial crisis.

The following is relevant to risk disclosure:

- Public companies should have a public risk profile. The profile should set out their key risks to attract investors with a risk tolerance to suit.

- The threshold of disclosure could be what investors would reasonably need to know about an investment's risks in order to make an informed decision.

- Industry standard(s), similar to the accounting standards, should be set up to guide the creation of key risk profiles.

- Risk profiles should be subject to sign-offs, audits and regulatory reviews.

- Regulators should have the power to prosecute companies for sub-standard risk profiles.

- Controls are used to stop downside risks from becoming reality. Control disclosures should be optional, depending on investors, the law and trade secrecy.

- Public risk profiles may push companies to develop innovative controls and sell their skills to investors.

- Financial losses should be reported to investors at a threshold set by the board and made public. Investors generally do not need to know about minor losses.

Chapter Twenty
Monetary Policy

Inflation is the rate at which prices rise. *Monetary policy* is a process by which many governments try to control it. They use the supply of money and other levers to influence the interest rates at which banks can lend. The size of these rates then affects the demand for loans, economic activity, the pressure for price rises and so inflation. Monetary policy is also a fairly blunt instrument as each bank is treated the same.

My suggestion is that banks should be treated differently according to their lending practices and risk profiles. Monetary policy should be used to discourage excessive risk-taking that fuels inflation as well as the next financial crisis.

Inflation

Before we go any further, it would be useful to talk about the problem of inflation a little more. Governments around the world hate inflation, which is understandable because price rises reduce the value of money. That is, money buys less and less as prices rise. The harmful effects include:

- Savings are worth less.
- Incomes are worth less.
- Retailers may raise prices to protect their incomes, which customers cannot afford.
- Workers may seek pay rises, which their employers cannot afford.
- Banks may increase interest rates to protect their incomes, which borrowers cannot afford.
- Fewer new loans / less economic activity.
- Fewer long term contracts / less economic activity.
- Investment is discouraged.

- Investors lose confidence in the currency.
- Long term productivity declines.
- Economic growth may be unsustainable.

Governments can control inflation by cutting how much they spend at home. If less money flows through the economy it may reduce demand and so price rises. This can cost them votes, however.

In addition, governments can give themselves the power to change interest rates. An increased rate will increase borrowing costs, reduce economic activity and so inflation may decline. This too is politically unpopular. It is also open to manipulation around elections and may lead to even worse economic outcomes.

The solution in recent years has been to give an independent body, such as a central bank, the power to set or influence interest rates. It makes decisions based on the rate of inflation, not political pressure. It may also help a government to explain why spending must be cut as well.

Monetary Policy

Governments use monetary policy to fight inflation. Typically they set an inflation target, such as 2-3%. Then the central bank is asked to maintain inflation within this target. The central bank should be independent of government interference in order to do so.[1]

Central banks use their role as banker to the *commercial banks,* which loan money to individuals and businesses, to put monetary policy into effect. They do so through buying and selling in the debt markets, together with short-term lending to commercial banks and influence. *Note: what follows is a simplified account.*

---

1 For further information, do an internet search for central bank websites, such as the Reserve Bank of New Zealand, Reserve Bank of Australia, US Federal Reserve, Bank of Canada, Bank of England or the European Central Bank.

The way it works is that the central bank first provides each commercial bank with a *settlement account*. These accounts are what the commercial banks use to deal with each other. For example, if someone pays you a cheque and your banks are different, the money will travel between their settlement accounts inside the central bank.

Second, the commercial banks must settle their accounts each day. This is also known as *balancing their books*. It means that the banks must add up all the money coming in and going out of their account with the central bank. If the daily outflows happen to be more than the inflow then the bank will have a deficit. They will have to borrow money in the *overnight cash market* to make up the difference. The interest rate that gets charged is called the *overnight cash rate*. But if the bank has a surplus, then they may lend it out overnight and make some money.

Third, the central bank influences the overnight cash rate by buying and selling financial products in the overnight cash market. There are different products, but they are a form of lending for the short term.[2] The more products that the central bank buys, the lower the supply of money, the more competition there will be and so the overnight rate will tend to rise. Likewise, the more that the central bank sells, the greater the supply of money, the less competition there will be for funds and so the overnight rate should fall.

The central bank's actions affect the overnight cash rate or rate of interest that commercial banks will have to pay if they need to borrow after balancing their books. To help matters along, the central bank will announce a target rate every month. They then buy and sell to reach this target in the overnight cash market. In fact, the central

____

2 The jargon varies and these products may also be called financial assets or securities. They may be issued by the central bank, depending on the rules in each country.

bank may be so powerful that it just has to announce the overnight rate it wants and the market will follow suit.

Fourth, the central bank influences the overnight cash rate because they are the *lender of last resort* to the commercial banks. So if a bank needs to borrow money overnight and can't get it on the overnight cash market, they can go to the central bank for an overnight loan. The idea is that this happens rarely, but if it does the central bank will lend at the rate it wants to achieve. This also influences the rates for the overnight cash market.

The action of the central bank in the overnight cash market has broader effects. The less money that is supplied and the higher the overnight cash rate, the more that banks will seek their funding elsewhere. It may mean there is more competition between banks for other funds. This pushes the price up, but if banks pay more then they charge us more. So interest rates go up generally. Of course, if we have to pay more for borrowing then we borrow less, spend less and economic activity declines. That then reduces inflation, which is what the central bank wants.

If economic activity slows too much then it may hurt the economy. No growth is harmful too. The compromise is that the central banks target an inflation rate that allows for some inflation and growth. Remember the inflation target of 2-3% that I mentioned at the beginning? It implies that some inflation (less than 2%) is OK. Central banks have a difficult job to get the balance right.

The central bank may loosen up if inflation is under control. It may announce a lower overnight cash rate target and supply more money again to the overnight cash market. If banks can then obtain more funds cheaply there, then they should compete less for funds. Interest rates should therefore fall, leading to more loans, more economic activity and more inflation.

Revised Monetary Policy

The overnight cash rate used by central banks is a fairly blunt instrument by which to influence inflation. A flat rate treats each bank as though they all have the same risks. This might be broadly true for one night, but not in the longer term.

Suppose that a bank decided to lend more money to riskier businesses in order to build market share. These riskier borrowers could use the money to expand and survive longer than they might otherwise have done. But high risk-taking in the economy can be disastrous when the economic cycle turns for the worse. These borrowers may be more likely to collapse and bring down others with them. Both the expansion and collapse will have an effect on inflation: price instability, the exact opposite of what a central bank is supposed to achieve. Yet banks are charged the same overnight cash rate even if their lending practices are quite different.

Governments may respond to a financial collapse by increased spending or guarantees for banks. Central banks may lower their inflation target. Yet these actions may fuel another cycle of inflation with the same result and the country becomes worse off.

A solution is that the central bank monitors not just inflation in the economy, but the risk profile of each commercial bank. As mentioned in the last chapter, these profiles, and the processes that create them, should be subject to audits and regulatory oversight. This should mean that the profiles are reasonably reliable. The banking regulator could also provide confidential reports to the central bank about how well each bank manages its' risks.[3]

Next, the central bank should charge a *separate overnight cash rate for each commercial bank every month*. This rate would be made up of a benchmark interest rate and a risk premium interest rate.

---

3 An information-sharing agreement may be needed, if one does not already exist.

- The *benchmark rate* would be charged to all banks according to the rate of inflation. The rate would be achieved by the central bank in the overnight cash market, as now.

- The *premium rate* could be a small amount of interest that is added to the benchmark rate. The rate could be an arbitrary percentage or something more complicated.[4] It would vary according to the central bank's assessment of each commercial bank's risk profile and information from its' auditors and the banking regulator (see below). It would also apply to loans made by the central bank as the lender of last resort.

It needs to be made clear that the premium rate should not be a sizeable penalty. Otherwise, the effect would be more competition for funds, both in and outside of the overnight cash market. That could push up interest rates to some extent and mean that other banks, their borrowers and investors could bear part of the cost. Instead, the premium rate must be nominal figure that is large enough to be noticeable and a signal of risk.

An important audience for the central bank's signals would be the international debt markets. Many commercial banks seek to borrow money there in order to lend at home. These international lenders charge different rates to banks already. The question is whether a premium would give an official signal that affected these international rates.

Suppose that the international debt markets saw a commercial bank as a having relatively low risk profile.

---

4 A discount on the benchmark cash rate could be used as well. So banks with lower risks would get a larger discount. This might involve the issue of discount debt securities in the overnight cash market that have a repurchase agreement built into them. However, I have referred to a premium throughout this chapter for simplicity.

If the central bank increased that bank's risk premium they might change their minds. International lenders could then charge the bank a higher interest rate (when it borrowed money to lend to others). The result would harm that bank's business. It would have to pass on the cost to customers and so lose business and investors. Or it would have to cut dividends and also lose investors.

The media, fund managers and investors could react badly to an increased risk premium. They might even sell shares in the bank in anticipation of worse performance. The incentive for a bank to build a riskier loan portfolio could therefore disappear.

On the other hand, some banks could still make high risk loans and be willing to bear higher funding costs. One reason could be that their investors agree with the strategy, even though it means higher funding costs for the bank, so they get a lower dividend. Or the bank may have a source of cheap funding, like a broad base of retail deposits. Then they can ignore the central bank's signal.

Of course, the banking regulator that watches over banks would watch each risk premium too.[5] If there were a long-term increase in premium, the regulator could require the bank to hold more capital for emergencies. It must be noted that a capital increase would be a much more drastic outcome than a higher risk premium. The scale of capital involved and the signal to international debt markets and investors would mean that the impacts for the bank would be negative. *Therefore, a rising risk premium trend could serve as an early warning of unpleasant downstream effects.* Investors in banks may not react kindly to this trend even if the debt markets were neutral in the short term (which I doubt). It could help to deter excessive risk-taking by banks.

The result of a revised monetary policy could be more stable banks, lower inflation and economic growth that

5 This regulator could be part of the central bank or a separate body, depending on the laws in each country.

is sustainable. Long-term investors would benefit if there were fewer collapses and if the value of their investments was eroded less by inflation. Short-term investors could still find opportunities though. For example, they could trade on the news of an increased risk premium according to their view of the commercial bank and its' risks.

Banking Practices

The revision to monetary policy outlined here could flow through to how banks lend to companies. It could address a problem where banks are under pressure to make quick lending decisions. They want to offer a the loan to suitable customers before their competitors. This can lead to too much reliance on numbers like earnings and profits. True, these numbers allow the fast comparison of companies and a quick decision. Financial ratios may also be used for the same reason (see appendix four for some examples). The danger is that the lender may not fully understand the operational risks of an industry or a company and make a poor lending decision.

One solution is to employ industry specialists, but there are recruitment costs. It may be cheaper just to use the numbers that are ready to hand. But what if the borrowers, at least *public companies*, already had an *audited* risk profile available? Would banks use it as part of the loan application **assessment**? I suspect so. This process might even expose borrowers who have under-estimated their risks compared to similar borrowers who are on the bank's books. It might cause the bank to seek more information from the borrower or review the loan. The bank might even need to report the profile to the relevant regulator if it breached any risk disclosure laws.

If banks collected risk profiles from their corporate customers, it could make it easier to create their own profile.[6] They could get a better sense of when and why

6 An extension of this approach would be to collect and review the risk profiles of material suppliers and joint-venture partners too.

these companies may not repay their loans. But if banks then under-reported their risks it would be more obvious too. The banking regulator or auditors should spot that the risks of a sample of borrowers were higher than those of the bank. This could lead to an investigation of how the bank used the risk profiles of its' borrowers.

In the worst case, the bank's profile would breach a risk disclosure law and could lead to a lawsuit. The banking regulator should also let the central bank and commercial bank know if an increase in capital is under consideration. Auditors should let the central bank and banking regulator know of any adverse findings as well. *Therefore, checks and balances can be created to stop banks from under-reporting their risks to reduce their overnight cash rate premium.*

A proposal to use different cash rates for commercial banks is not as unusual as it may first seem. The international debt markets already charge different interest rates to banks, as noted above. Banks also charge different rates to customers. For example, corporate borrowers who have difficulty repaying their loan may be charged a higher rate of interest. This is compensation for their increased credit risk and is a form of 'pricing for risk'. Banks should not complain if the central bank were to take a similar approach with them. It seems fair to me.

In conclusion, others will know better than me if a rising risk premium would cause a bank to collapse. I doubt it, but it would depend on the size of the premium. I suspect instead that risk management would become even more of a necessity than it is already.[7]

Summary

Not all banks are equal, yet they may be treated so under a nation's monetary policy. In my opinion, the overnight cash rate used by central banks to control

---

7 In an emergency, other measures may also be available, such as government support for the bank.

inflation is too blunt. It could be improved by adding a premium over the benchmark cash rate that reflects the risk profile of each bank. This in turn may influence the cost of funding for banks and so quickly reduce the value of taking more and more risks. The public would benefit generally if greater price stability were to result and economic growth were more sustainable. For example, savings and income would erode at a slower rate. Fewer businesses may fail. The long-term growth of investments could prosper.[8]

The proposal made here comes with a large assumption: that the international debt markets that fund banks would be influenced by a premium for risk as part of the overnight cash rate. I cannot say for sure if this would actually happen. However, it seems likely as debt markets are much more sensitive to risk following a global financial crisis. Even if the markets were neutral, a bank that is charged a high risk premium could be required to hold more capital for emergencies in due course. Banks and their shareholders should be sensitive to that outcome, even if they took notice of nothing else.

I think that the proposal made in this chapter is worth further consideration. (My apologies if there are boxes of academic work on it already). It makes me doubt whether another option, a general rise in the capital held by banks, is really needed. Surely banks could put this money to better use in funding economic growth? But after a financial crisis, banks first need to reassure investors that they really have paid enough attention to their risks.

---

8 I doubt if stagnation would occur for reasons such as new fashions, new technology, climate change, natural disasters, etc.

Chapter Twenty One
Risk and Reward

Some people in public companies are paid to take risks, even though it might not be put like that. They are the leaders who decide which projects and products to fund. Risk-takers are also the traders who invest surplus money in the market. Their decisions will flow through to company profits and their bonuses. It is a system that can encourage risk-taking behaviour.

The trouble with risk-taking is that the long-term effects can be harmful. There is not much point making a gigantic profit in one year if you enter a loss for the next five as a result. It is therefore worth looking at pay packages and how risk-takers are rewarded.

My proposal in this chapter is that risk-takers in public companies[1] should be paid in line with profits and downside risks. To do so, I will take a closer look at developments with the Basel Capital Accord. This is the international agreement that requires banks to hold capital for emergencies (see chapter fifteen). It uses a mechanism to calculate capital that can be applied to the bonus payments of risk-takers.

The Revised Basel Capital Accord

The revised Basel Capital Accord presents an interesting connection between risk and returns in banks.[2] Risks may be assessed through industry research, loss data, workshops with staff and professional opinion, etc. Banks may employ risk advisers to assist them. The result is a bank risk profile with a focus on downside risks.

In addition, a dollar value is given to the overall risk

---

1 As before, I refer to public companies for simplicity, but my comments may also apply to other investments.
2 This was not entirely new. Some banks pioneered the connection between risk and return long before the Accord was first issued.

profile, based on impacts and likelihoods. Some banks may add rigour with complex mathematical models, but the inputs and interpretation are still going to be matters of opinion. Even so, the result should be reasonably consistent with practice, audits and oversight by the banking regulator. The result is a dollar value for downside risk that informs the amount of capital which each bank must hold for emergencies.

At a more detailed level, banks consist of divisions, containing different lines of business, each with its' own risks. The bank capital can be split across these divisions according to their risks.[3] For example, divisional net profit = gross earnings minus costs, interest charges, tax and a divisional capital amount. There can be complications, but the result should be net profits that are adjusted for risk. These are a form of *risk-weighted return*.

Important note: the calculation and use of capital and the capital charge are complex issues. Different countries may also use different regulatory approaches. The account given here is therefore highly simplified, at the risk of over-simplification.

The divisional returns may look quite different when risk is taken into account. A division may have a high income in one year, but if there are high risks then the risk-weighted returns could be very low. The bank board may prefer to fund the divisional businesses with lower gross returns, but much less risk in the long term.

Bankers with a high tolerance for risk will probably hate their divisional capital amount. The more risk they take to increase earnings, the higher this amount will be. Their risk-weighted net profit may therefore even fall. If they do nothing, then earnings could decline or risks rise

---

3 A number of activities could be captured through this process due to their impact on risk. They includes product design, manufacture, restructures, outsourcing, mergers and takeovers etc, etc.

anyway with the same result. The board could decide to give the division less funds, sell it or shut it down. The same approach could be taken for business lines within each division too. It squeezes the banker between profit targets and risk consequences. Banking has become a lot harder.

It may be asked why the revised Basel Capital Accord did not stop the global financial crisis. First, it was issued in 2004 and not all banks had adopted it, or finished putting it into operation. That comment also covers an application to staff rewards (below). Second, it could take years before the experience of risk assessments, loss reporting and so on becomes effective. Third, different risk assessment methods are used under the Accord. The standard of assessment may need to be raised in due course. There may also be other reasons, but it is hard to know since bank risk profiles are not made public.

Other Risk-Weighted Returns

There is potential for a similar process of risk assessments to be used in public companies which are not banks. A dollar value for risk could be produced as above. The difference is that this amount would be *synthetic*, or exist only on paper, not as capital that it must put aside. Yet the company could use a synthetic capital amount for the same purpose: to guide future business decisions.[4] These decisions would be more informed by longer-term risk, so that returns become more sustainable.

A question will arise whether all public companies should disclose their risk-weighted returns. There could be benefits if they did. Investors could use this data to assess how key risks impact on earnings and whether that outcome suits their risk tolerance. For example, Fundamental Analysts could use these returns as part of sensitivity analysis (see chapter twelve). Investors

4 Exceptions could include companies without income, like mining explorers and early stage ventures.

could also use the reported figures to compare the risk management performance of competitors. How investors react could help to drive risk management within these companies. Therefore, I suggest that *all public companies should be required by law to disclose their predicted and actual risk-weighted returns*. It could serve as an extension to profit reporting and the public disclosure of their risk profile.

Risk-Weighted Rewards

Now we come to the pointy end of this chapter: staff rewards. I will assume that many business people, particularly in management, get paid a combination of fixed salary and a flexible bonus. I will also assume that the size of that bonus depends on performance that is linked to certain Key Performance Indicators (KPIs). Typically, the measures relate to targets for earnings, profits, cost management, market share and so forth. Softer measures may also come into play like team leadership, complaint rates, etc. Risk management could be added too.

Any KPI that is based on financial performance could have a risk component in the form of a target for risk-weighted returns. As a result, high earnings growth with even higher risks may not result in a large bonus. This is because those earnings may not be sustainable if the risks are so high. A similar approach could be applied to the release of directors' stock options.

I do not believe that all staff should have their bonus weighted for risk. It should only apply to the chairperson, directors, the chief executive officer, divisional leaders, traders and other risk-takers. I do not expect these people, often Big Business types, to change unless they are hit in the wallet. For example, would some have stocked up on credit derivatives, where the risks far exceeded the profits, if executive bonuses were shredded as a result?

I think not.

In addition, earnings will often fall in a recession, but risks may not fall as fast. This may be because risks are something akin to a fixed overhead, so if the company is in a certain business it will always have risks that come with it. As a result, risk-weighted returns could fall sharply. Bonuses would therefore fall too. This could be the answer to public anger when directors are paid well in a financial crisis.

A rewards system that incorporates risk is important after a recession. As the economy recovers, profits may grow without too much work by management or directors. If bonuses are just linked to annual profit growth then it may deliver a windfall that is not deserved. However, the increase in the size of risk-weighted returns may not be so great or meet the KPI target. More effort would be needed before bonuses returned to their previous levels. It seems fair to me.

The exact wording of a KPI will be confidential, depending on your local law. But it is pointless to have separate KPIs for profits and risk. It is too easy to favour earnings performance and give too much leniency for the risks that were taken. That is why profits and risk should be combined as a risk-weighted return. Therefore, *public companies should be required by law to use risk-weighted returns in relevant KPIs, even if the details are not made public.*

Two checks on the use of KPIs are obvious. First, the company would still need to report on the overall risk-weighted returns, as proposed above. The company may not meet its targets if the KPIs were not managed properly. Second, it has been proposed that the company publish a risk profile that is audited (see chapter nineteen). This audit could include a review of a sample of KPIs for relevant people in the company to check if they meet the legal requirements.

It must be admitted that a few staff may deliberately under-report their risks. They could make false risk assessments or do poor research (due diligence) on complex products, like mortgage-backed securities and credit derivatives (see appendix five and six). It would be much easier for these staff to meet their risk-weighted targets if they lied about the risks. But if the result was a larger bonus it would be a form of *fraud*. Dismissal and even prosecution could follow audits and regulator investigations. The company could also be sued for a risk profile that was not true and fair, or whatever standard was used in local law. Checks and balances could therefore be built into the rewards system.[5]

I am confident that changes in risk-taking behaviour can occur. In particular, Big Business types are highly adaptable and will compete anywhere. But if Big Business people were put off by a new rewards system, others may find room at the table. It could add to any movement to increase the diversity of skills and experience on company boards and in leadership teams. The glass ceiling would crack, but the results are impossible to predict.

Summary

Under the revised Basel Capital Accord, banks must assess their risks. The outcome is a dollar figure that banks can use to risk-weight their financial results. This approach could reveal how high earnings can come with even higher risks. It may be preferable to fund activities with lower earnings, but lower risks over the long term. The same approach could be used for other public companies which are not banks. The results could be more sustainable and reduce the risk of another global financial crisis.

The disclosure of risk-weighted returns should be

---

5 It may also lead to a shift from bonuses to higher salaries, unless shareholders or law-markers prefer that the payments are linked to risk management.

required by law for all public companies.[6] Investors could use it to compare the performance of different companies. Their risk tolerance and reaction could the help to drive risk management within these companies.

An interesting application of risk-weighted returns is the use in staff rewards. Companies may set Key Performance Indicators (KPIs) using targets for risk-weighted returns. The bonus paid to staff would then reflect the risks that they take, not just profits. It follows that this system should be limited to risk-takers in the company, such as the chairperson, directors, chief executive officer, divisional leaders, traders and so forth.

Audits and other measures can be used to ensure that risk are not under-reported by a few to improve their results and get a larger bonus. Individuals who did so could be prosecuted for fraud. The company could also be prosecuted for sub-standard risk disclosures to investors.

---

6 A possible exception is mining explorers and others without current income.

Chapter Twenty Two
Corporate Ethics and Culture

Ethics is a name for moral ideas of right and wrong. Most of us know what they are, but what one person thinks is right and wrong may be slightly different to another. To make matters worse, ethics exists in the context of culture, another term that is hard to define. One way of putting it is that *culture* links a group of people with a common understanding and patterns of behaviour. Ethics is part of that understanding and patterns of behaviour flow from it.

I think it is reasonable to assume that all investors want corporate ethics and culture that promote risk management. Some suggestions are made here on how companies can meet this demand. Once again I will refer to public companies for simplicity, but this chapter is applicable to other investments as well.

Corporate Culture

It is fair to say that corporate culture interests most directors and senior executives. A common set of values and behaviours in an organisation Is a fantastic way to deliver on a company strategy. It is cheap since people will act without being asked. It also great if the culture then meets the expectations of the company's customers and shareholders. They gain a sense of comfort that leads to repeat business or long-term investment.

On the other hand, culture can hinder a strategy that does not fit. It is pointless to try and get bureaucrats to become free-wheeling entrepreneurs. Or try to get folks who make like to make decisions as a group to follow a hierarchy. They will resist the changes and leaders who hold a different view. The company would be better to improve what they have. My understanding is that there are three main influences on culture that can be used to improve it: top-down, side-ways and outside influences.

Top-Down Influence

Company leaders create the *top-down influence* on culture. It is delivered in speeches to staff, through Key Performance Indicators, websites, press releases and marketing. In fact, everything the chairperson, directors, chief executive officer and executive team say or do has an impact. This applies to small business leaders too.

My suggestion is that leaders include their own ethical views as part of their normal communications with staff members. The content should be:

- Personal
- Real-life
- Short

Personal stories are particularly useful if staff are interested in their leader and what motivates them. Real-life stories grab attention, like current events (eg. court convictions), company strengths and weaknesses. It will reflect the risk tolerance of the leader, including their upbringing and family values. But the stories also need to be short. The audience may be time-poor, restless and probably will not want a sermon. Shorter stories may also be absorbed without the staff thinking too much. They will simply know what is expected and get on with their work. (Children's games which teach morals should be avoided unless *all* the staff enjoy that sort of thing).

Side-Ways Influence

A *side-ways influence* on culture is that of the peer group. Co-workers can be agents for change inside a company.[1] Any form of interaction between them can be used to promote similar behaviours and avoid extremes. How ethics are discussed and how often is up to the company (another top-down influence). But it *must allow*

---

1 An industry standard is another side-ways influence on culture, but I doubt if it is as powerful as peer pressure.

all staff members to contribute. Input will come from Big Business types, Intellectuals, Small Business types and Team Players. It will reflect their combined risk tolerance and community values. The result will help to deliver the company plan.

Leaders need to know if their strategy can be implemented or if it will be undermined. Smart leaders will pay attention to what their staff believe and their values. In this way, staff may influence their leaders, including those who suffer from moral lapses.

Outside Influence

There are many *outside influences* on corporate culture. Religious leaders, politicians, judges, regulators and consumers are important. Yet they may not have the same prominence in the company calendar as investors.[2] Furthermore, the influence of investors may be felt quickly through changes in share price and market trends. Plus investors own the company after all, fund new ideas and pay bonuses. This is why the law reforms in this book aim to make more use of investors. It is through them and their collective risk tolerance that the needs and values of the community may influence each company.

Whistleblowers

There are dangers for leaders and staff if they make ethical statements. First, it might be tough to do if they built a career by walking over others. Second, if they present a moral face, but act differently, whistleblowers could appear.

Whistleblowing is a practice that got a boost after the collapse on Enron Corporation in the USA in 2001. A staff member who reported irregular practices before the

---

2 It is possible that consumers will have the same level of influence in a small company. In a large company it is unlikely that the same consumers will be shared across different divisions and products. The major outside influence in that case will be shared investors.

collapse was apparently told off. So now there are laws in many countries to protect and encourage staff who wish to 'blow the whistle' on fraud, corruption or other wrong-doing. These laws, depending on how they are written, may uphold the right of staff to speak with management, auditors and regulators.

Retaliation within companies should be banned. But I doubt if the whistleblower laws are that effective on their own. There are too many ways to retaliate against these people that are difficult to prove. Whistleblowers may need more motivation to come forward (other than envy or ego). I mean the fury of someone who hears a leader or team say one thing and do another. Even the best people could make this sort of mistake, but if *corruption* is involved then more staff should speak up.

Culture of Compliance

There is an Australian law that which has potential to support corporate culture. Companies may use culture like a character reference when they break the law. This is turn could drive them to improve their culture. Something like it could be adopted elsewhere, at least for public companies.

The Criminal Code Act applies additional penalties to the breach of a range of Federal Australian laws. Buried in the Act is a couple of legal tests that use corporate culture as a means to assess fault.[3] A judge must consider if a corporate culture existed that "directed, encouraged, tolerated or led to non-compliance" with the relevant law. Another test is whether the body corporate failed to create and maintain a "corporate culture that required compliance". These tests therefore give the judge a broad discretion to assess corporate culture and the role of management.

To be honest, it does not appear that the culture of

---

3 Paragraphs 12.3(2)(c), (d) Schedule to the Criminal Code Act 1995 (*Commonwealth of Australia*).

compliance tests have had that much use. However, the Australian Securities and Investments Commission found that a bank had a "poor compliance culture" relating to its' role in the collapse of a securities lender. The regulator stated that "deficiencies in processes were not identified, escalated or remediated in an appropriate or timely manner".[4] In that case a deal was done outside of court, so the legal tests were not used by a judge. It seems to be only a matter of time before these tests are more fully applied.

How far the judge investigates will depend on the nature of the law system in each country. The evidence will likely be a mix of risk profiles, processes and the behaviours associated with them, as well as evidence of how a culture of compliance was built inside the firm.[5]

If the judge found a risk profile to be misleading, they may consider the history of risk assessments that fed into it. A pattern of non-compliance with an industry standard for risk profiles (see chapter nineteen) would obviously indicate a weak culture of compliance.

In addition, a judge may look at a breach of the law in the context of how the company managed its' risks. A pattern of problems could point to a culture that at least tolerated the breach, even if it did not directly cause it. For example, there may have been inadequate funding, many control gaps, numerous errors and losses, failures to report or fix problems. The judge may then find that there was a weak culture of compliance.

---

4 Australian Securities and Investments Commission (6 March 2009) "Opes Prime: Proposed Settlement and ANZ Enforceable Undertaking", Media Release 09037, www.asic.gov.au.
5 Some may prefer that the term 'risk management culture' is used. This would suit those who see compliance as a sub-set of operational risk. In fact, operational risk is becoming a sub-set of compliance as risk management is regulated more. There may also be less discretion with compliance decisions and a greater focus on the ethics that underpins the law than with operational risk generally. This is desirable, so I prefer to use 'culture of compliance'

Evidence of culture-building within a firm could support the company. It could be used to suggest that a breach of the law and minor weaknesses are exceptions rather than a pattern. To this end, the firm could demonstrate the top-down, side-ways and outside influences on their culture. A company with a rigid hierarchy or one with a dominant leader may favour more top-down influences. A consensus or innovative one may prefer side-ways influences. All should be influenced by investors.

Evidence for a culture of compliance should, in my opinion, act like a character reference. If a judge decided that a company has a weak culture of compliance, it could imply that it is unlikely to learn from its mistakes. A larger penalty could then be needed as a punishment and deterrent. For example, a large penalty may be warranted for misleading risk disclosures that were based on a pattern of failures and deceptions. In contrast, a simple error in a risk profile may be seen as such and not something more sinister. Culture may therefore be used to calm those who see every mistake as being connected.

In addition, it would be useful to *extend the culture of compliance tests to senior executives in each company.* I suggest the chief executive officer and their executive team since they have the biggest top-down influences on culture. The culture of compliance tests could then apply to a law they broke at work (eg. a decision which breached a company licence). The tests should make a difference as to whether they were jailed, for how long they were jailed, if they were fined or how much they were fined. The penalties could be severe. It would remind these executives how much they *really* value a culture of compliance.

If the tests were extended to senior executives, the evidence of culture-building, or a lack of it, would become even more important. Examples of weaknesses include a leader who has no personal involvement with their emails to staff. Or there may be staff policies, but no means to find out if they are read. A set of management models won't help either. Leaders who tell everyone that they lead by example sound really, really weak to me. I doubt if that line would hold up in court by itself.

Better evidence would come from a collection of sources. For example, brief records of top-down efforts, performance review notes, board resolutions and team meeting minutes (though it will not be practical to collect the minutes throughout a large company). Together it could form a corporate diary of actions and outcomes. This evidence could be used to counter examples of a weak culture of compliance. It may also reveal if the ethics of the leadership and staff are not in sync. For example, it could create whistleblowers if the staff have better ethics. Alternatively, it may show how the leaders inspire their staff or at least keep the toe-suckers in line.

Company leaders make seek guidance for how to build their corporate culture. One approach is to create an official list of proper behaviours, like those used in the US Federal Sentencing Guidelines.[6] The problem is that it could be used as a checklist, which is so broad that it is easily met or so detailed that gaps occur. Companies may just take what they do already and fit it to this list. *Change will not happen.*

For the same reason, it would be helpful if judges used their discretion and did not endorse any risk specific management process or behaviour. That could just lead to a checklist put together from different judgements. Again, change will not happen.

My preference is for examples of weaknesses, like those given by the UK Financial Services Authority.[7]

---

6 United States Government (2009) Chapter 8B2.1, Effective Compliance and Ethics Program, Federal Sentencing Guidelines: www. ussc.gov.

7 Financial Services Authority (2007) "Treating Customers Fairly - Culture". www.fsa.gov.uk.

These examples could be used in industry guidance that is not binding.[8] Company leaders would still gain a sense of what to avoid, but be left to *improve their strengths in risk management*. They must find their own path, provided it does not lead back to court. *Otherwise, changes will not come from within, be genuine or sustainable.*

Fit and Proper

In another development, ethical tests have been set for selected persons in regulated financial services organisations.[9] Words like honesty, integrity, reputation, competence and capability are used. Some of these issues may be satisfied by qualifications and work experience, but others are ethical standards. These standards could affect whether someone is hired or removed from a role. The culprits may even be banned by the regulator from similar roles. After a global financial crisis it might be asked if this 'Fit and Proper' test, or at least the ethical part of it, should be applied to the leadership of all public companies.

One problem is that someone may commit an offence in their private life that has nothing to do with their business role and potentially be sacked or banned. However, this makes sense if you believe that their choices in one area could affect their business decisions.

Another problem is that ethical standards are open to interpretation. Unfortunately, there is no ruler with honesty and integrity stamped on it. Most of us would be reluctant to destroy someone's career unless we were really certain of their foul play. Yet if foul play is certain (eg. murder, fraud, breach of director duties, parking fines etc.), then surely a breach of the law could be proved in

---

8 In contrast, a standard for risk profiles would need to be compulsory if it dealt with common classification issues.

9 Financial Services Authority (2004), Chapter 2, Main Assessment Criteria, in "The Fit and Proper Test for Approved Persons", FSA Handbook, Release 027: www.fsa.gov.uk; Australian Prudential Regulation Authority (2008) APS 520 Fit and Proper: www.apra.gov.au.

court. Would not a court order to sack or ban them be more appropriate? A Fit and Proper test would not add anything in that case.

If nothing can be proved in court (or a conviction has nothing to do with their role), we must use our personal ethical standards, on a case-by-case basis. Yet these standards may differ inside companies or within regulators, particularly when dealing with low-level issues. Who then in their right mind is going to *explicitly* reject a job candidate or sack someone under a Fit and Proper test? It is not worth being hit with a law suit (if that option exists). Again, a Fit and Proper test would not add anything.

The result could be an official checklist and a review that is compliance-on-paper. For example, just ask everyone if they had good morals during the year and see what comes back. I doubt if serious matters would be reported unless the police were already aware of them. The least serious are probably open to debate, as above.

Ethical reviews might not succeed even if they are thorough. For example, a leader could have an impeccable reputation (as evidence of their ethics), but still be rotten. Indeed, Bernie Madoff was widely respected until it was found out that he ran a gigantic Ponzi scheme.[10] Madoff's reputation was partly how he gained new investors and avoided detection for so many years. So a review of his reputation probably would not have been that useful. (Other regulatory checks could have got him though).

In addition, international co-operation is needed to put a Fit and Proper test into effect. The impact of a ban is weakened if the person is able to move overseas and start again. But international arguments could then develop about what the ethical parts of 'Fit and Proper' really mean. Plus a bureaucracy would be needed to deal

10 A *Ponzi scheme* is a fraud where returns to investors are paid out of new contributions rather than earnings.

with any foreign bans or international law suits. I don't think it would be worth the cost.

For the reasons outlined above, I am not in favour of the ethical component of a Fit and Proper test being applied to business leaders generally. My preference is for other measures in this chapter. Rather than just look at the actions of individuals, and get bogged down in their ethics or lack of them, we should focus on individual action in the context of culture. This is the overall pattern of behaviour inside a company, which is based on ethics. A Fit and Proper test is not needed for this to happen.

A corporate culture that is weak will fail to deal with small frauds or other foul play. But if early action is taken, like dismissal and prosecution, it may stop the development of problems that are big enough to bring down a company like Enron. Big Business people who 'grow up' in a culture of compliance should *implicitly* recognise others with the same values and hire them. It is this sense of 'fit' that is used along with qualifications and experience for the job. It is not easily conveyed in evidence, except indirectly through the use of risk management processes, evidence of culture-building and so a culture of compliance.

Summary

Ethics is a broad topic that covers moral standards. Some of these ideas, like honesty and integrity, are difficult to define when you look at them closely. This can make it hard to decide what is ethical in some cases. (Clear examples of unethical behaviour or foul play can of course be dealt with). However, personal ethics contributes to how people, and the companies they work for, behave. Together, these common behaviours in a company are known as corporate culture. It can be more useful to look at these patterns of ethical behaviour than get bogged down in a discussion about individual ethics.

Corporate culture is useful because it can be reviewed in a court of law. If a breach of the law exists, a judge may then look at the culture in which it happened. How risks and errors were found and dealt with inside the company will be important. Evidence of culture-building will also be important. The judge may then get a sense of how seriously compliance with the law was taken, whether the breach was an isolated error and how likely it is to be repeated. A strong culture could therefore lead to reduced penalties (depending on the nature of the breaches).

An official list of what makes a strong culture of compliance should be avoided. Otherwise, people will rely on it rather than developing corporate culture from within. Companies and senior executives should instead be put on the spot. Their legal liability should be linked to uncertainty about how their employees will behave. One solution is for them to drive a culture of compliance from within, which is genuine and sustainable. For them it is a form of personal risk management.

A culture of compliance is important for investors, particularly if public risk profiles were to be required by law. A strong culture would support the delivery of a risk profile and encourage more informed decisions (see chapter nineteen). A strong culture would also support changes that promote sustainable growth (see chapters twenty and twenty one). Investors could therefore welcome measures to improve corporate culture. For example:

- Leaders should take personal accountability for building ethics in their organisations. To be effective, their communications on ethics should be personal, from real-life and short.

- Staff members should contribute their ethical views to the delivery of the company plan.

- Legal tests should be used to assess the culture of compliance in companies. Evidence of culture-building within a company is important.

- Corporate culture should be promoted from within. External standards may not be as effective.

The legal tests are the key suggestion, as the accountability for culture and the power to assess it are set in law. Use of these tests may stimulate feedback from investors in the market and affect the company share price. Maximum leeway is given for leaders to respond, get involved and improve their corporate culture from within.

If the corporate culture or the evidence of it is weak, then at least more staff should become whistleblowers. Corrupt leaders and teams who say one thing and do another may offend the genuine whistleblower so much that they are prepared to do something about it. Their evidence may even contribute to the assessment of corporate culture in court.

Chapter Twenty Three
Reform

Law reforms should encourage investors to give feedback about company risk management and culture.[1] This feedback will differ if companies attract investors with different risk tolerances. Even so, company leaders who are concerned about how their investors will act will make improvements. Then the risk tolerance of leaders and investors should become better aligned. Feedback could be encouraged as follows:

- Greater risk disclosure (chapter nineteen) would give investors more information with which to judge public companies. Companies may be encouraged to sell their skills in risk management as a brand. Investors will pay more for shares in a company that they trust.

- Central banks could charge an overnight cash rate according to the risk profile of each bank (chapter twenty). It could send a signal to international lenders about a bank's risks. This signal could influence each bank's funding costs, its' lending practices and the risk management practices of its' borrowers. Investors would provide their feedback in the sharemarket.

- Risk-weighted returns (chapter twenty one) are a way to assess the downstream effects of corporate decisions. They would affect the allocation of internal funding and individual rewards. The publication of risk-weighted targets and results would be judged by investors.

1 As before, I refer to public companies for simplicity, but the suggestions could be applied more broadly.

- The culture of compliance could be used as a form of character reference for companies and senior executives who break the law (chapter twenty two). The law could include the proposals made above. Failures in risk management could lead to serious penalties if the culture of compliance were found to be weak. Investors may react badly if they fear that other risk management failures could also exist.

If these reforms were adopted, it would channel investor pressure to each stage of the business, from strategic decisions and funding to performance, review and reward. The advantage of doing so would be to challenge any cultural barriers to risk management that exist. These barriers could arise from the huge investor pressure on public companies to improve their performance every year. That pressure may lead to an emphasis on short-term decisions. In contrast, the reforms proposed above encourage feedback on the long-term effects of short-term decisions. This could produce business decisions that are more sustainable.

The problem with the reforms is that many steps are involved, like the assessment of different risks. Much can go wrong and often does. Yet the company leadership cannot be everywhere or know everything. Leaders may be uncertain about what their staff are really doing. Their personal liability may intensify that uncertainty.

The solution is for the leaders of public companies to actively build a culture of compliance. As a result, their staff should comply with the law reforms and fix errors as they happen. But these benefits should also flow through to risk management and positive investor feedback.[2] The result should be a repeating, strengthening cycle. It is how we will avoid another global financial crisis and repair the damage that has already been done.

---

2 There are other benefits too, like compliance with the financial reporting laws, consumer protection laws and more.

The suggested reforms should not be considered alone. There are important checks and balances that can be used. Some of these are:

- Competition to develop innovative controls.

- Competition to sell a company's risk management skills to shareholders.

- A trusted culture is a brand that is valuable to gain and too valuable to lose.

- Audits and regulatory visits to vet risk profiles and Key Performance Indicators (KPIs).

- Independent risk advisers who do not report to the management whom they advise.

- Commercial incentives exist for banks to use the risk profiles provided by borrowers.

- Auditors and regulators could compare a bank's risk profile with those of its' borrowers. They could identify if a bank has under-reported its' risks.

- The banking regulator could inform the central bank if any bank under-reports its' risks.

- The banking regulator could make banks hold more capital for emergencies if their risks rise.

- The debt markets will form their own view of a bank's risk profile and lend accordingly.

- Public companies could be prosecuted if their risk profiles are sub-standard.

- Individual staff could be prosecuted for fraud if they under-reported risks to get a larger bonus.

- Whistleblowers may be encouraged if leaders and teams promote ethics, but act corruptly.

- Regulator funds must increase with growth in what they are required to police.

- Regulator powers must be balanced by the legal right of companies to achieve their objectives in an efficient way.

The last point is critical if more law and regulation is to be adopted. Companies must have the legal right to act in an efficient way. Otherwise, government bureaucracy, policies, visits and demands for information can get out of hand. What then is efficient? It is difficult to say precisely. The basic idea of increased efficiency is that you get more output from what you put in. To complicate matters, efficiency also varies, so change the law and you will change what is efficient under that law.

If you find the idea of efficiency confusing, there is a simpler approach. Just remember that costs are inefficiencies. So for a *company to act in an efficient way it will need to keep its' costs down*. Part four is about how companies may reduce their long-term costs. But a *regulator must also consider the costs to business of its' actions. This is how a regulator will help businesses to achieve their objectives in an efficient way.* I think that *all* regulators need this check included by law to protect businesses from regulatory overkill.

An example already exists in Australian privacy law. The Federal Privacy Commissioner must act with consideration for the right of Australian businesses to achieve their objectives in an efficient way.[3] It means a

3 See section 29(a) of the Privacy Act 1988 (*Commonwealth of*

balance is needed between regulatory action and the cost to companies.

Some regulators may turn the issue around. They may ask businesses to prove that the costs of regulation are excessive before they are prepared to ease up. For a small company it might be easy enough to create a list of costs. It will be harder for a larger company to do so. A large company may spread the workload across more staff, so has to split up the time and salaries that are spent on regulation. It will not be an easy task where the company is like a small city. IT changes can also be difficult to price if not all of them are due to regulation. Then there are the costs of documentation (including the destruction of outdated material), education, project managers, etc. But companies should not have to hire bureaucrats to prove the obvious: regulation can cost a lot to implement and follow.

The practical solution is for regulators to employ staff with commercial experience. It means that they can target regulation, time their visits or requests for information much better, if they do not do so already. It also means that regulators must be funded sufficiently to afford this commercial experience. It does not mean the avoidance of regulation (sorry). Nor does it mean that the parties will always agree.

The suggestions made in part four may not be the best or only ones. For example, the power of banking and

---

Australia):

> "In the performance of his or her functions, and the exercise of his or her powers, under this Act, the Commissioner shall:
> (a) have due regard for the protection of important human rights and social interests.... and recognition of the right of government and business to achieve their objectives in an efficient way."

The Commissioner also regulates how certain Australian government agencies handle private information. The reference to government shows that business has not been given special treatment.

company regulators could be increased. Banks could be required to hold more capital for emergencies. Conglomerates could be split to limit insider trading. But if there are no cultural improvements from the *inside* it is unlikely that there will be any real change. *Management will instead be challenged to seek out unregulated risks*. History will repeat itself yet again.

In contrast, the suggestions made in this part offer another path to the repeat of history. Cultural and risk management improvements should be made with investor feedback in mind. In my opinion, this is how the business community will avoid the most costly outcomes, like prosecutions, class action lawsuits or insolvency. It is also how law reforms may avoid creating a false sense of security or *moral hazard*.

What I have not covered is how investment styles and strategies have a role to play too. For that I must briefly revisit all four parts of this book and bring them together in a final conclusion.

Conclusion

It is impossible for me to end this book without commenting that investment is all about opinion. Your view of your investment personality is opinion, your risk tolerance, goals, strengths and weaknesses are all matters of opinion. Which strategies you choose and how you use them is opinion. This whole book is opinion.

One benefit of seeing everything as opinion is that it is open to question. Just because the market might, say, be dominated by long term investors with a leaning toward Fundamental Analysis, it does not mean they are right. True, if there are large numbers of investors with a similar outlook they can drive the market. But weight of numbers does not mean that there is a best way to invest or an ideal risk tolerance level. We are much more complicated than that.

A diversity of opinion makes sense to me. Team leaders know, or are trained to know, that an effective team is made up of people with different skills and abilities. This is useful because we do not know everything. We therefore need teams with complementary skills. They will include the Big Business, Intellectual, Small Business and Team Player personalities.

If this team example is applied to the marketplace, then it is important to have a wide range of investors with different risk tolerances and strategies. Together, a large number of investors, and the community they represent, can have a powerful effect on public companies.[1] Smart leaders appreciate the risk tolerance of their shareholder base and it should influence their risk management practices. After all, directors must keep their shareholder's confidence if they want to keep their capital or seek more of it.

____

1 Once again I refer to public companies for simplicity. My comments could also apply to other investments too.

Governments should make more of the diverse investor base that exists or could exist. They should legally require all public companies to disclose key risks and risk-weighted returns to investors. In doing so, unsustainable profits may be exposed, leading to better strategies and bonus payments.

Collectively, the risks of companies should flow through to the risk profiles of the banks that lend to them. It should affect each bank's risk profile, the cost for it to raise funds and flow back to borrowers as interest rates. This in turn may affect market prices and hedge spreads. The outcome should be an incredibly diverse series of risk assessments, risk management, information flows and feedback, involving an equally diverse investor base.

Investors should not wait for their government to fix everything in a crisis. It is possible to look *within* at your personality and risk tolerance. This knowledge can be used to refine your goals, build strengths and limit weaknesses. It can also be used to select an investment strategy that is right for you, including the timeframe, risk analysis and risk management methods. Really these are just means to reduce the costs of an uncertain world, a world of risk, and so create more confidence. Something similar happens in business through risk management and in government through the law. Together we may not achieve the best outcome, whatever it is, but we may avoid the most costly outcomes.

Please do not misunderstand me. I am in no way pushing an alternative to moral standards or religion. But it would be good to give business leaders more support, particularly a few who work on the margins of morality. I mean support from a culture of compliance, which is influenced by the ethics of their staff and investors, and which is backed by the courts. It is about giving these leaders a strong moral compass and kicking them if they do not follow it.

As I write, world leaders are still grappling with how to deal with the fall-out from a global financial crisis. It is the product of a loss of trust and confidence in markets, companies and governments, so that uncertainty is revealed. More laws and regulation are on the way as a result. It may calm the public who have been reminded that we live in a world of risk. But nothing will really improve unless there are also cultural improvements within companies and the depth of investor talent is better tapped. This is not the sole responsibility of investors, companies or governments. We have a shared responsibility.

Appendix One
Problem Gambling

Problem gambling is the product of a chemical addiction, not a high risk tolerance. The chemical is called *dopamine*, which excites our brain nerve cells and makes us feel happy. Dopamine has widespread uses: it may be released during gambling as well as exercise, pain, sexual intercourse, eating or as a result of using certain drugs. The desire for dopamine can become a need for gamblers that drives their behaviour. In fact, dopamine addition is a form of mental illness. This is why I did not include problem gambling as a weakness in chapter nine.

In theory, investors may become problem gamblers too. It may start with successful investments and the pleasure of winning. Then losses follow, the investor spends more to recover their stake and a cycle of self-deception begins. Dopamine addiction could develop and so investment risk may be ignored, misinterpreted or not identified at all. The investors probably do not understand that their decisions have become irrational.

Addiction can creep up on you, but there may be warning signs as well as solutions. It is beyond the scope of this book to discuss them in detail, but here are some key questions from an internet website:[1]

- Have you ever skipped work or study to gamble?
- Have you ever missed an important event so you could gamble?
- Have you ever bet more than you could afford?
- Have you ever used money set aside for food bills to gamble?
- Do you try to win back the money you have lost?
- Have you ever been in an argument with friends or family over gambling?

---

1 www.problemgambling.vic.gov.au

- Have you ever gambled to escape from things that are causing you stress?
- Do you find you are gambling on your own more and more regularly?

It is recommended on this site that if you have answered "yes" to a number of these questions then you should seek help. Access is provided to a counselling service. Other charities may exist in your area which fulfil the same role.

Now look again at the list above and substitute the words "invest / investing / invested" for "gamble / gambling /gambled / bet". Did you answer "yes" to a number of these questions? If so, then you potentially might have a gambling problem where the market is your casino, race track or lottery machine. Your judgement may be distorted by an addiction. However, I am not an addiction counsellor and cannot diagnose or advise you. If you have any questions or concerns about problem gambling you should seek advice from a qualified professional.

Appendix Two
Stress and Worse

Stress is a fact of life, so it might seem like a waste of time to have an appendix on this subject. But investors do not live in a social vacuum either and should consider the effects of their stress on others as well as themselves. The following warning signs are taken from the internet:[1]

Warning signs of immobilising stress:

- *Physical: Diarrhoea, constipation, IBS* [irritable bowel syndrome], *back pain, breathing problems, migraines, insomnia, low libido, a disrupted menstrual cycle.*

- *Emotional: Constant worrying, anxiety, feeling everything is out of your control and you are trapped.*

- *Behavioural: Mood swings, tantrums, constant fidgeting, withdrawal from normal life.*

What is a breakdown?
The term actually refers to a wide range of experiences when someone has hit rock bottom. There is no such thing in medical terms, and making a diagnosis based on such a flimsy term is near impossible.

- *Severe depression: This is the most common type of breakdown, where someone develops severe depression over a few weeks, where they can't sleep, feel on edge, have negative thoughts about themselves, feel more and more hopeless and then one day just can't get out of bed.*

- *Collapse in social roles: Inability to keep doing day-to-day job and playing your usual part in family/ social life.*

---

1 www.thesite.org.

- *Loss of sense of reality: When the person becomes delusional, 'has lost the plot'. A psychotic breakdown, although this is not always indicative of schizophrenia.*

The site on which I found this information recommends medication and a coping strategy, either through group or individual therapy.

Suicide

In the most extreme scenario, investment failures may lead to suicide. It is a desperate response to losses that hurt self-esteem, reputation, community standing and families. Suicide is the biggest loss of all and gives away your opportunity to rebound.

The Samaritans, a charitable organisation, have listed some suicide warning signs.[2] Some of these signs may also occur for other reasons.

(a) Emotional Warning Signs

- Feeling distant from others, outside looking in.
- Extreme tension in their bodies.
- Flashes of themselves taking their own life.
- Funeral fantasies.
- High anxiety.
- Fear of themselves.
- Thoughts that repeat in a circular fashion.
- Seeing no meaning in life.
- Afraid of being alone.
- Lack of motivation.
- A sense of guilt that leads to fear of discovery.
- Difficulty concentrating.
- Lost interest in things without developing new interests.
- Too much or not enough sleep.
- Desire to use alcohol and/or other drugs to escape

---

2 www.thesamaritans.org.au

from discomfort.
- Belief that they are unlovable or evil.
- Powerful fear of losing love.

(b) Behavioral Signs
- Making plans to depart such as giving away important possessions and saying implicit good byes.
- Isolation from family and friends.
- Loss of interest in career or study.
- Sudden mood changes.
- Taking up or changing patterns of substance use.
- Apathy about appearance and hygiene or extreme fastidiousness.
- Sudden mood changes.
- Sudden calm after anxious state.
- Risk taking behaviours.
- Low energy and lack of motivation.
- Physical withdrawal from touch.
- Changes in eating patterns (overeating or loss of appetite).

Similar information may also be found elsewhere and recommend that you seek out qualified professionals for prayer, counselling, medication or other services. At least you may need to review your investments and strategy in order to find a different, less stressful approach.

Appendix Three
Indices

A *financial index* is a compilation of market data. Movements and trends in the indices can generate signals for the investor and contribute to their view of risk, whether market risk or related to economic issues. Here are some examples of indices. The financial press or internet may be a starting place to look for others.

(a) LIBOR

The *London Interbank Offered Rate* (LIBOR) is known as the primary benchmark for interest rates. It reflects the rates at which banks lend money to each other in London for periods of up to a year. This has a flow-on effect for interest rates worldwide given the large number of banks involved. The trend in the LIBOR is therefore a general signal for interest rate movements.

In addition, the LIBOR is used around the world as a reference rate. For example, it may be used to calculate the interest payments on certain debt securities that are listed on an exchange. So the LIBOR trend may influence the market price for these securities too.

(b) TED Spread

The *TED Spread* is the difference between the interest on certain US government debt and the interbank market. It is represented by the 3-month US Treasury Bill (T Bill) and 3-month LIBOR. A rising spread may indicate that commercial banks have more credit risk so they charge each other more for debt (The T Bill is assumed to be risk-free). It may also indicate that money is being withdrawn from the interbank market. The TED spread reached record levels in late 2008.[1]

---

1 See Krishna Guha, Michael Mackenzie and Gillian Tate (18 September 2008) "Panic Grips Credit Markets", *Financial Times*: www.

(c) MSCI

The *Morgan Stanley Capital International Index (MSCI)* tracks the biggest companies in the most developed economies. Size is measured by *market capitalisation*, which is a combination of the value of the stocks and the number of shares.

Investors and fund managers may base their portfolios on the companies that make up this index in the belief that the largest will perform the best over time. As a result, the entry or exit of a stock from this index can have a significant effect on its' market price. If the stock enters the MSCI, it may push up its' price. Likewise, exiting the MSCI could push the stock price down further.

(d) Country-specific Indices

Indices are often country specific. In Australia, for example, various indices are produced by Standards & Poor and the Australian Stock Exchange.[2] These comprise stocks selected by a committee according to their size and liquidity. The indices cover different categories of large, medium and small market capitalisation or particular businesses such as metals and mining. An understanding of the overall trend for an index can help investors and analysts predict future gains and losses in the market or industry.

(e) Futures indices

A *future* is a contract to buy or sell an asset for a set amount and price on a future day. An index derived from the prices of certain futures can be used to predict market movements. Or how market players believe it will move. For example, changes to a futures index related to debt instruments may reflect expected changes in yields.

---

ft.com

2 See www.asx.com.au/research/indices

(f) VIX

The *Chicago Board Options Exchange Volatility Index* (VIX) is a useful indicator of market uncertainty.[3] It is calculated from the market price of certain options with 30 days until expiry (see appendix six about options). The reason for using options is that investors use them to protect themselves against risk. So if the prices of these options rise, it may be linked to an increase in the price volatility for the underlying securities, uncertainty and an increase in investment risk.

The VIX tends to rise in times of panic, so it is also known as the investor fear gauge. Conversely it tends to fall when the market advances, though it is not fool-proof. The VIX also has value for investors around the world, as volatility in America can spill-over to other markets.

---

3 See www.cboe.com

Appendix Four
Financial Ratios

A *financial ratio* is simply the relationship between certain numbers. The numbers used may include the market price for that investment and/or reported financial data, such as earnings, costs, profits, debt levels, interest payments, prices and so forth (see examples below).

Ratios are a well-known source of information for share analysis, but can be used for other investments to some extent. Don't be put off by the calculations. They are fairly straightforward once you have chosen your favourites and have had practice. Companies and brokers will often calculate them for you.

An advantage of a ratio is that it integrates a huge amount of data into one number. That number then can be used to compare performance for an investment over a period or to compare different investments easily. Investors can therefore tell at a glance something about these investments. It not only saves research time, it can let investors make quick decisions in response to news.

A key disadvantage of financial ratios is that they represent a snapshot that is soon outdated. A solution is to use ratios as guidance or in addition to other measures, like an assessment of management or economic conditions. However, ratios based on market data, like bond yields, will fluctuate and give more useful trend information.

Another disadvantage of ratios is that different calculation methods can produce different results. So if you are using the same ratio, you need to ensure that you put together the source data (eg. earnings) consistently. However, there is no guarantee that companies interpret the accounting standards in the same way. This will affect their data and your financial ratios. Some variation seems to be inevitable and may need more research.

Examples of Financial Ratios

The rest of this appendix contains a list of some of the more common ratios. If you are interested in financial ratios, then I encourage you to do more research on the topic. An internet search could be a starting point.

Note: the following examples use division ("/"means "divided by"). That is, do the division in the brackets first.

(a) Current Yield: is used to price interest-bearing debt. It is calculated by the interest rate (coupon) divided by the market price of the debt, multiplied by 100 to give a percentage. The current yield is constantly changing with movements in debt market prices.

Current Yield =(Interest Rate/ Market Price) x 100

If the credit rating of the debt issuer improves, then the market price for that debt may rise. If the debt is a fixed rate bond, then the current yield will fall. That is, the same rate / higher market price = smaller yield.

(b) Debt to Equity: is typically the amount of capital raised through debt compared to what Is raised from equity, such as shares. Debt to Equity is calculated from the total debt divided by the total equity.

Debt to Equity = Total Debt / Total Equity

A low debt to equity ratio could mean that a company is financially conservative and gets a lot of its capital from shareholders. But in a crisis, it could mean that borrowing it just too expensive and issuing shares is cheaper. A problem with this solution is that the dividends must be shared out between more shareholders (diluted). Other ratios, such as Earnings Per Share (below) could worsen as a result.

(c) Discount Yield: is used to price *discount debt*. The borrower receives less than the full value of the debt (the discount), but pays back the full amount at maturity. The difference is lender's profit. The discount yield is then the discount divided by the purchase amount, multiplied by 100 to give a percentage.

$$\textbf{Discount Yield = (Discount / Price) x 100}$$

A more complicated calculation is needed to price the discount if the period of the debt it is not for a full year. It must be adjusted for the difference.

(d) Dividend Cover: is the number of times that net earnings or profit can cover (pay for) dividends to shareholders. The dividend cover is calculated from the net profit divided by the dividend payment (per share).

$$\textbf{Dividend Cover = Net Profit / Dividend Paid}$$

The higher the dividend cover, the more money that a company has left over after paying out dividends. Whether this is seen as good or bad will depend on the company and its needs, either to keep reserves or to reinvest for future growth.

(e) Dividend Yield: is the proportion of dividend income relative to a share investment. The dividend yield is calculated from the dividend (per share) divided by the share price and multiplied by 100 to give a percentage. The dividend used may be the most recent historical figures, projected dividend or a combination (choose the dividend consistently to avoid distortions).

$$\textbf{Dividend Yield = (Dividends / Share Price) x 100}$$

The higher the yield, the cheaper the shares may be relative to the dividend. If the yield is rising, it could mean the shares are a bargain. Or it could just mean that the market has concerns about the stock.

(f) Earnings per Share (EPS): is an indication of potential dividend payments. Earnings per Share is the net earnings for a period, divided by the number of shares in the same period. The EPS may need to be adjusted if the number of shares change in the period.

EPS = Net Earnings / Total shares

(g) Interest Cover: is the number of times that earnings can cover (pay for) interest payments. Interest cover is calculated from the earnings before interest and tax (EBIT) divided by the interest payments (per share) for the same period.

Interest Cover = EBIT / Net Interest Payments

The lower the interest cover, the more concern an investor may have that the company will not be able to service its debts. It may become critical with higher interest rates during a credit crunch.

(h) Net Profit Margin: is a measure of how much profit a company has made from its sales, expressed as a percentage. Net profit margin is the net profit (after all expenses and losses) divided by sales and multiplied by 100.

Net Profit Margin = (Net Profit/ Sales) x 100

The Net Profit Margin is particularly useful for comparing retail operators such as supermarkets. A company that outperforms the market again and again may have competitive advantages that need to be understood.

(i) Net Tangible Assets (NTA): is a measure of the underlying value of the company or book value. Net Tangible Assets are calculated from the total value of all assets with the value of intangible assets (eg. goodwill) subtracted.

NTA = Total Assets - Intangibles

(j) Net Tangible Assets (NTA) Per Share: also known as **Net Tangible Asset Backing**. It is a measure of share worth if all the assets were sold. It can show if the stock is a bargain relative to the value of its assets. It is calculated from the NTA divided by the number of shares on issue.

NTA Per Share = NTA/ Share Number

(k) Return on Equity (ROE): is a broad measure of how well an investment has performed given what was raised from investors or equity. A high ROE can indicate a growth stock with strong earnings and profit growth.

ROE = (Net Income/ Total Equity) x 100

(l) Working Capital Ratio: is also known as the **Current Ratio.** It is used to assess if a company can pay its short term debts using assets like cash or those that can be readily turned into cash. The Working Capital Ratio is calculated from the current assets (eg. cash) divided by the current liabilities.

Working Capital = Current Assets/ Current Liabilities

A more accurate version of this ratio excludes

inventories from the current assets because they cannot be sold quickly to pay debt. Overdraft facilities may also be excluded from current liabilities if it can be extended. However, the calculation method should be the same to avoid distortions.

The size of the ratio and whether it is viewed as good or bad will depend on the company and industry. The more working capital that is needed to fund a business, the higher the Working Capital Ratio will be.

(m) Yield to Maturity (YTM): gives the value of a debt instrument that bears interest. It is calculated from the interest rate, current market price and the time remaining until maturity.

Appendix Five
Mortgage-Backed Securities

Banks with a lot of home loans may make their regulator uneasy. The reason is that these banks can be too exposed if borrowers cannot repay their debt in a financial crisis. There are various solutions. The bank may sell the risk of default to others (see credit derivatives, appendix six). Another solution is to offer some of its' home loans to investors as mortgage-backed securities.[1] These securities are a way for lenders to show that they can raise more money if they need to, as well as sell the risk to others.

Normally, mortgage-backed securities would not form part of a general book. They are complex products and bought by large institutional investors. But these securities, designed partly to reduce risk for lenders, actually contributed to the global financial crisis. Investors therefore need to know a bit about them.

Securitisation

The way *mortgage-backed securities* work is that a lender sells the right to receive mortgage payments to a third party investor. However, the title to the house is not sold and the home owner may be unaware of the deal. If the home owner then defaults on the loan, the lender will follow normal procedures, including selling the house. But the investor will bear the loss if the loan cannot be repaid. As a result, *credit risk is transferred to the investor.*

The process by which mortgage-backed securities are put together and sold is called *securitisation*. A bundle of loans that belong to the same lender are combined into a pool or group. The lender issues an offer document, which

---

1 There are many other structures possible, for example those which use payments from corporate debt, bonds or derivatives. Each has its' own jargon and supporters.

sets out how payments are backed by the mortgages and any other details. Investors tender for a portion of that loan pool. Obviously, they will prefer loans with a low credit risk, so may rely on the report of an independent rating agency. Finally a contract is agreed between the parties. The price of a mortgage-backed security is then the cost of the original loan, a portion of the expected profit that the lender would have received, plus any other fees.

Note the lender still keeps a portion of the profit. It means that they make less per loan, but regain all their capital to loan out again. The lender should be able to make more loans and so make more profit overall. Securitisation is therefore a business model, not just a means to reduce risk.

Crisis

Securitisation was supposed to convince regulators that banks could raise money in a crisis. Unfortunately it did not work out like that when all the banks shared the same crisis. The problem was even worse for non-bank lenders that were funded by securitisation.

The fear was that too many high risk loans could default at once, which the investors could not bear. The matter was complicated by the complexity of some products and also the potential scale of risk exposure. It contributed to a loss of confidence and the market for mortgage-backed securities died.

Actually, there is nothing wrong with securitisation. It is how it is managed that is the issue. Stricter regulation of rating agencies could help, as would better quality risk assessments by some lenders. Mortgage-backed securities are still useful.

Appendix Six
Common Derivatives

Derivatives are a contract related to an underlying asset (eg. shares and bonds) or an indicator (eg. indices and exchange rates). I have set out some common types of derivative below and how they are used. If you want to know more, there are plenty of textbooks, education courses and mathematical pricing models out there. An internet search could be a useful starting point.

Futures

A *future* is a contract for the sale of an asset at a set amount and price on a future day. So if you buy a future, you buy the right to delivery of that contract. Examples of assets include wheat, gold or fatty pork products. You can also buy a future for delivery on some intangible matter like interest rates. However, the future in those cases will be delivered in cash rather than a physical commodity.

Forwards

A *forward* is a more specialised type of future. They are used to sell the rights to future production. For example, farmers use forwards to sell their future crop or animals. The money the farmers receive then can be used as working capital used to buy seed for new crops, breeding stock and pesticides. Miners also use forwards to sell future ore production. Again, the money is used as working capital, in this case to fund the mine operation.

A problem for producers is that they need to deliver on the contract even if they produce less than expected. For example, weather or disease can hurt farm production, or mines may have lower quality ore than the miner thought. The cost of buying extra assets on market to meet their obligations can be very expensive.

The upside of forwards (and futures generally) for

investors is that the market price may rise higher than the contracted price. By buying the derivative, investors therefore get the assets more cheaply than if they bought later in the year. The downside is that the asset prices can fall and their derivatives will then be worthless. The opposite is therefore true for the sellers, like farmers and miners. If prices fall, it means their incomes are protected and so selling the forward was a good move.

A problem for investors is that some futures and forwards may be structured so the set price and the actual market price are compared regularly. The difference or *margin* needs to be paid by the loser to the winner. Over time these payments can add up and become dangerous for the loser. The cost can be extreme and so these derivatives are generally avoided by beginners and those with limited capital.

Options

An *option* is a standardised contract that comes with the right to trade in a specific security before a certain date. It is therefore like a future, except that it comes with the option to transact. Options give the owner the right to buy or sell once a price threshold has passed: the *strike price*.

Call options give the right to buy. *Put options* give the right to sell. However, all options expire, so if you have not made money by this date then your investment will be lost. At least you know the maximum impact of your potential loss: it was what you paid for the option.

For company shares, call options make money if the share price rises above the strike price. Likewise, put options make money if the share price falls below the strike price. The winners should be able to re-sell their options on market, provided there a buyer.

Other assets could in theory be optioned too, including the right to buy or sell property units or even other derivatives. The trigger may be a price or an economic indicator like an index level, interest rate threshold.

Investors could use options to speculate on future share prices. Or they could *hedge* the risks of part of their portfolio by taking an opposite position. For example, you may own shares and risk losing money if the share price falls. But if you buy put options for those shares, then you will make money if the share price falls below the strike price. In this way, your potential loss is hedged.

Warrants

Warrants are a form of long-dated option, so many of the comments made above apply. A warrant is a contract to buy or sell a shares at a specific price, but at a future date that may be many years from now.

A warning: you need to examine the terms and conditions of the warrant very carefully as there may be a lot of variation. For example:

- The number of warrants that are packaged together can vary, unlike options that tend to have a standard number. This means unwary investors can buy what looks like a bargain, but actually delivers less than they think.

- Warrants may exist for the same assets, but the terms differ between issuers.

- Warrants may be exercised on the expiry date or earlier, depending on the market.

- Some warrants may come with a sale price that is guaranteed. So if the warrant loses money then you will get your investment back. This insurance is not free, of course. These warrants may be more expensive than others, but deliver more as well.

Swaps

A *swap* is an agreement to exchange the cash-flows from different investments. These investments may be *synthetic*, or made-up, in order to standardise their features. The idea is that there will only be a few differences that reflect the different risks of each investments. In this way, investors agree to exchange these risks.

For example, investors may each hold a bond of same duration and rate, but one produces income payments in US Dollars and the other in Euros. The value of the swap will therefore depend on the US$: Euro exchange rate. If the US dollar falls, the value from the swapped Euros will increase (and vice versa). The investors have therefore swapped currency risk. This kind of swap could be purchased by importers and exporters. If their business income fell due to the exchange rate, then they should have a corresponding increase in income from a swap with the opposite exposure.

The size of the risk associated with a swap can be limited partly by the number that are bought. However, the loss on each swap can be open-ended in terms of the cashflows. Therefore, swaps are generally avoided by beginners.

Credit Derivatives

A *credit derivative* is used to reduce the risk that a borrower won't pay back their loan. The structure of credit derivatives can be complex. Some are in the form of swaps. Effectively the lender uses a derivative to pay a third party to take the credit risk of each loan. It is like buying insurance. If the borrower defaults, then the third party must pay back the loan instead. This ought to give confidence that the lender will survive a wave of loan defaults, which the third parties hope will never happen, but it did.

Too many inferior loans were made before the

global financial crisis started in 2007. That is, the borrowers had a high credit risk and too many defaulted when the crisis hit. The investors in credit derivatives could not pay back the loans either. Panic followed, which was partly due to the scale of credit derivative exposures and fear about what would happen. Banks would not lend to each other, or at extremely high rates, because they did not know if they would get their money back.

Like mortgage-backed securities (see appendix five), there is nothing fundamentally wrong with credit derivatives. They fulfil a legitimate role in the market, but improvements in corporate risk management are needed (for example, the proposals made in part four).

Selected Further Reading

These books were sources, influences or just interesting:

Futures Stock (1980) by Stephen Calder, Patrick Lindsay & David Koch, Castle Books.

Gods Of Management (1995) by Charles Handy, Arrow Books.

Institutions, Institutional Change and Economic Performance (1990) by Douglass C. North, Cambridge University Press.

It's Your Life. What Are You Going To Do With It? Coach Yourself (2001) by Anthony M. Grant and Jane Greene, Pearson Education Limited.

Rich Dad's Guide To Investing (2000) by Robert Kiyosaki and Sharon Lechter, TechPress.

Share Investing For Dummies (2002) by James Dunn, Wiley.

The Art of Possibility (2002) by Rosamund Stone Zander and Benjamin Zander, Penguin Books.

The Complete Idiot's Guide To Making Money On Wall Street, third edition (2000) by Christy Heady, Alpha Books.

The Essays Of Warren Buffett: Lessons for Investors and Managers (1999) by Lawrence A. Cunningham, Wrightbooks.[1]

The Sneetches And Other Stories (1961) by Dr Seuss, Random House.

Working with Monsters: How to Identify and Protect Yourself from the Workplace Psychopath (2005) by Dr John Clarke, Random House Australia.

---

1 See also www.berkshirehathaway.com

Made in the USA
Lexington, KY
01 June 2010